THE PROCESS OF RECONCILIATION WITHIN THE LITHUANIAN CATHOLIC CHURCH: AFTER THE SOVIET OCCUPATION

THE PROCESS OF RECONCILIATION WITHIN THE LITHUANIAN CATHOLIC CHURCH: AFTER THE SOVIET OCCUPATION

Rimantas Gudelis

Foreword by
Robert J. Schreiter, C.PP.S.

Lithuanian Research and Studies Center
Chicago
2002

THE PROCESS OF RECONCILIATION WITHIN THE LITHUANIAN CATHOLIC CHURCH: AFTER THE SOVIET OCCUPATION

By Rimantas Gudelis

Library of Congress Control Number: 2002107659
ISBN: 0-929700-38-4

Published by
Lithuanian Research and Studies Center, Inc.
5600 South Claremont Avenue
Chicago, IL 60636-1039 USA
Tel. (773) 434-4545
Fax (773) 434-9363

TO MY BELOVED PARENTS AND
IN LOVING MEMORY OF MY GRANDPARENTS
ALL OF WHOM SPENT MANY YEARS IN SIBERIAN EXILE

ACKNOWLEDGMENTS

First I am grateful to God that during the years of Soviet occupation I was able to become acquainted with and participate in the underground activities of the Catholic Church of Lithuania and to meet many incredible people who, by example of their selflessness, taught me to love God and country, to love the truth, and to detest evil.

I want to sincerely thank all the dissidents who agreed to participate in this project and grant interviews. I thank them for their openness in discussing the very sensitive and timely topic of reconciliation. It is most unfortunate that due to the sensitivity of this subject matter I am unable to mention them by name. Also wishing to remain nameless are those who helped guide me through the labyrinth of the KGB archives. I also thank the Center for Religious Studies at the University of Vilnius for allowing me to make use of collected interviews with noted dissidents for their project "Transition and Hope." My thanks to the Lithuanian Research and Studies Center in Chicago and to its staff for providing me access to their archives and libraries, which helped greatly in my work. My sincere thanks to Dr. Jonas A. Rackauskas for his invaluable comments and suggestions.

I am very grateful to the faculty, staff and students at the Catholic Theological Union for their constant support, friendship and concern that made my study there so enjoyable and meaningful.

While belonging to the underground of the Church in Lithuania we were taught not to learn people's last names in order to avoid betraying someone inadvertently during interrogations. In similar tradition I am unable to name those in Lithuania who assisted in this work. However, boldly and with deep respect I would like to acknowledge Herbert Anderson, John Linnen, Anthony Gittins, Stephan Bevans, and Mark Francis whose theological vision and teachings expanded my theological education invaluably and allowed me to delve more deeply into my work.

My extreme gratitude also goes to a number of individuals at the Catholic Theological Union: Dianne Bergant, director of the Joint Doctor of Ministry program, for her positive encouragement and support; special thanks go to Robert Schreiter for his wisdom, profound insights into key aspects of ministry and reconciliation, friendship and extremely valuable input all along the way. I would like to acknowledge Claude-Marie Barbour for her deep inputs about the process of reconciliation that flows from her life experience. I want to thank my colleagues, Jozo Grbes and Luis Vera whose advice and donated time contributed greatly to the completion of this work.

My thanks also to Rev. Vito Mikolaitis and Jack Irvin for their help with the English language.

VII

TABLE OF CONTENTS

FOREWORD

One of the most difficult challenges for the Church in the formerly Communist countries of Europe is achieving a moral reconstruction within the Church itself. At a time when the Church is called upon to help rebuild the larger society after decades of atheistic and authoritarian rule, the Church finds itself first confronted with the task of finding the healing needed within its own ranks. The situation varies considerably from country to country, but in nearly all instances there is a need to come to terms with a past which has damaged the internal life of the Church considerably.

That this is the case should not be surprising. The Church is a divine institution, but it is also a deeply human one. The issue is not only human weakness and sin; it is also about having to make decisions in difficult times, when the future is far from clear. People in the Church in Lithuania were confronted with all these difficult issues. Many suffered deeply for the decisions which they made. Now, in a time of reconstruction, those who suffered for their faith must be honored. And at the same time, the Church needs to move forward into a new kind of society.

What has become evident in situation after situation around the world too is that skills for leadership in a time of resistance do not always translate well into a new situation of reconstruction. This is particularly painful for those who gave so much to keep the faith alive under extremely difficult circumstances. The reconstruction of the life of the Church, especially for the new generation coming of age, requires a careful balance of remembering the past and preparing for a different kind of future.

This book by Father Rimantas Gudelis is a contribution to that work of reconstruction of the Catholic Church in Lithuania. Drawing upon his own experience in the concluding years of Communist rule in Lithuania, and upon the experience of churches in other countries struggling with similar issues of remembering, healing, and reconciliation, he offers a number of things which will be valuable for the Church in Lithuania as it struggles to move forward.

First of all, he reconstructs the history of the Soviet attempts to crush religion in Lithuania, and the role of the dissident movement in resisting those attempts. One of the first things which has to be done in efforts at reconciliation is to establish as clearly as possible the truth about the past. There will always be competing versions of that past. But an effort must be made to state the case as clearly as possible from the point of view of the victims, since a Catholic understanding of reconciliation holds that God begins the healing process by engaging the victims. It is the healing of the victims which creates an environment in which the deeds of the wrongdoers can be confronted and dealt with. Father Gudelis tries, first of all, to reconstruct the fifty years of history as the backdrop against which efforts at reconciliation and reconstruction are to be understood and undertaken.

Second, he retrieves the stories of the former dissidents. This is an important next step in the reconciliation process. The accounts of those who risked much and suffered for their faith, and how they see prospects for reconciliation are the major ingredients in the first stages of the reconciliation process. What his interviews with the former dissidents revealed was the depths of pain still present in those who suffered, and the need to get a wider understanding of Catholic approaches to reconciliation and forgiveness.

In his third step, he turns to the rich resources of the Scriptures and Church tradition to bring forward what Christian faith has to offer to understanding reconciliation - both within the Church itself, and in the wider society. This wider understanding can help give the Church in Lithuania new resources by which it can honor those who have suffered, and find a way into a different kind of future.

Father Gudelis draws this all together to offer ways in which the Church might think differently about itself and act accordingly. One of the things which has been learned in other situations is that for reconciliation to happen, there have to be some fundamental shifts in thinking and acting. In efforts to reconstruct, we are inevitably drawn back to visions of the *status quo ante*, of trying to imagine the Church as it might have been before all the repression and suffering took place. Unfortunately, we cannot return to that place because the deeds of the past have marked us irrevocably. The question is, however, just how we will come to terms with that past. We cannot remain hostages to the past, but we cannot erase it from our memory either. We have to become, as St. Paul puts it, a "new creation." (2 Cor 5:17) The resources for that vision is the final thing which this book offers to us.

No two histories of suffering are ever alike. Nor are the pathways out of suffering into a reconciled future identical. That is why the careful work of telling the truth about the past, hearing the stories of those who suffered, and plumbing the resources of our faith will always be needed. This book offers a guide through all of this, not only for the Church in Lithuania, but also for others who are looking for parallel efforts which might illumine their own situation. Everyone in these kinds of situations is struggling to find a way forward. What Father Gudelis offers us here is an important help in this process now going on in so many countries, and of such great importance to living out the Gospel in the twenty-first century.

Robert Schreiter, C.PP.S.
Pentecost, 2002

INTRODUCTION

A. Origins of the Problem

This work flows from the author's ministerial experience extending through the period when the Lithuanian Church was oppressed, during the period of Gorbachov's *Perestroika* when society and the Church moved toward reconstruction, and in the current period of independence.

The author was involved in Church activities when he was in high school. He belonged to the underground organization Brothers of the Holy Eucharist (Eucharistijos bičiuliai)[1], which was a youth organization led by those opposed to the Soviet regime. He was also an altar boy in the diocesan cathedral, and it did not take long for him to discover that the Church was divided. The bishop and priests in the cathedral were defending "peace" as the Soviet regime wanted, which required that many compromises be made with the Soviets. During meetings with the Brothers of the Holy Eucharist, the leaders expressed different ideas as they opposed any kind of collaboration with the Soviet regime. During these meetings, they tried to show how unjust the Soviet system was and to build in the hearts of young people a love for the Church and the people of Lithuania. It was very clear that the Church was divided when the leaders of the Holy Eucharist organization warned us not to talk about our meetings with certain priests. All these meetings were held secretly. First, it seemed strange to hear the warning of not talking to some of the priests, but now that the codenames of the KGB for these priests are known it is very clear why these warnings were made. The Church was divided into two parts – those who decided to collaborate and those who did not.

When the author entered the seminary, the division was very clear. The seminarians who came with the protection of the KGB or promotion of the KGB collaborating pastors were different from the seminarians who had decided not to collaborate.

Later, when the author was ordained, his pastoral experience showed him how difficult are the times of transition, how difficult it is to move from resistance to the reconstruction of society. From the interviews with former dissidents, the author

---

[1] Underground Catholic youth movement in Lithuania founded by dissidents in 1969.

3

learned that many of them were still living the spirit of resistance. For many of them the theology of reconciliation and spirit of forgiveness to the former wrongdoers or for those who think differently from them was foreign.

From the author's studies at the Catholic Theological Union in Chicago, he learned that different churches have dealt with reconciliation within Church circles differently. In Russia where almost every bishop collaborated with the Soviets, there are no resources for the reconciliation process even to this day. In Poland or Eastern Germany, where just a few people within Church circles collaborated, those not holding high positions in the Church, the Church found it easier to deal with reconciliation by replacing the wrongdoers.

The Church in Argentina dealt differently with this problem than did the Church in Chile. Every case is different. There are some similarities between Lithuania and different countries but every case is unique, as in Lithuania where there were two groups within the Church – those Church officials who collaborated and those who resisted. Two strong opposite poles existed during the Soviet period of Lithuanian Church history. These two unreconciled groups still exist in the Lithuanian Catholic Church after more than ten years of independence. This says that the Church and society are not reconciled and that it is a long process, which needs to be studied and discussed.

B. Focus and Goal

The topic of this work is to explore the process of reconciliation in post-communist Lithuania. The biggest part of this study will address where the Lithuanian Catholic Church stands in this process. Because the Church during the Soviet period took a leading role against the Soviet occupation and atheization, many Church leaders were killed, imprisoned and persecuted, but some of them chose to collaborate with the Soviet government. The core of the study will be interviews with dissidents who resisted against the Soviet regime and how they now understand reconciliation in the Lithuanian Roman Catholic Church and society.

When we speak about dissidents, we have in mind the Lithuanian dissident movement within the Catholic Church, which began in the '70's. They organized their activities around three different groups: the Committee to Defend Catholic Rights in Lithuania, *The Chronicle of the Lithuanian Catholic Church*, which was the longest lasting underground publication in existence in the Soviet Union, and the Brothers of the Holy Eucharist, an underground organization to which the author belonged.

The dissidents who were most active during this resistance movement were interviewed. From these activities they gained an authoritative position among the

4

Lithuanian people during the Soviet regime. They all spent long years in the Soviet gulags. Due to the sensitivity of the subject matter, their names will not be revealed here. Also, the author is grateful to the Religious Studies Center at the University of Vilnius for allowing him to use their interviews with other noted dissidents, gathered during a joint project with the University of Vienna entitled "Transition and Hope." (Aufbruch)

The goal of this study is to help the Lithuanian dissident group and all Catholics to understand the theology and spirituality of reconciliation and to help develop a strategy within the Lithuanian Catholic Church towards forgiveness and reconciliation. One of the most important elements in seeking reconciliation after social conflict is telling the truth.

After the demise of Communism in Lithuania very little was said about what had happened. The truth about the wrongdoers was not told. At that time society and especially the Church, having suffered from the cruelest persecution, no longer had the strength to tell the truth, and after a time the wrongdoers even became "heroes" who were awarded medals of honor. At the same time they had privatized or embezzled a large portion of public property. In this way the victims of the Soviet regime were victimized a second time. A major obstacle in seeking reconciliation in the Lithuanian Church and society is telling the truth about the shortcomings of the past. For this reason we will discuss that which occurred during the years of Soviet occupation at some length.

Besides truth telling, the most helpful tools to move towards reconciliation are the theology of reconciliation, which is practically unknown in Lithuanian culture, and the experience of how different cultures and churches have dealt with the process of reconciliation in a post-oppression environment. We chose this approach because the author was part of the Church in resistance and also because the process of reconciliation always begins with the victim. If within the Lithuanian Catholic Church and society reconciliation is possible, we believe that the group who were dissidents (victims) should begin and lead the Church and society to reconciliation.

C. Method

This study uses the Whiteheads' method, inviting into a dialog the Christian tradition, personal experience, and cultural resources. We involve three steps – *attending, assertion*, and *pastoral response*.

Attending – means seeking out information on a particular pastoral concern (reconciliation) that is available in personal experience, Christian tradition, and cultural sources.[2] *Assertion* - Engage the information from these three sources in a process of mutual clarification and challenge in order to expand and deepen religious insight.

Pastoral response- Move from insight through decision to concrete pastoral action.[3]

In a Lithuanian context pastoral activities often seem separate from Scripture and tradition, and applied theology (the attempt to maintain a traditionalist focus and where social change is ignored) is dominant even these days. Not many ministries are paying attention to experience and culture in the Lithuanian Church. The Bible is understood as absolute and ahistorical. These two paragraphs from the Whiteheads' book *Method in Ministry* will help understand how, in a Lithuanian context, the method is applied:

> Turning to Scripture, we find again and again stories of faith as a journey. God has led our ancestors along strange paths and through circuitous routes toward grace and healing. These journeys have included long seasons in the desert; detours, dead-ends and bad judgments were part of these adventures. Jesus' own journey through death to new life included failure and public humiliation.
>
> Given the chance to reflect, we notice how our own lives echo and affirm these Scriptural accounts. We too are familiar with wrong turns, blind alleys, and missteps along the way. Attesting to this resonance between tradition and experience, our lives become further testimony, reinforcing- the scriptural account of faith.[4]

D. Ministerial and Theological Import

Past. From the past biblical texts will be cited that speak in favor of forgiveness and reconciliation as well as examples from Church history and tradition where the Church has many resources to deal with forgiveness and reconciliation.

Present. There is deep division within the Catholic Church of Lithuania. There is a great need to overcome this division. The former dissident group can play a

---

[2] James D. Whitehead and Evelyn Whitehead, *Method in Ministry* (Kansas City: Sheed & Ward, 1995), 13.

[3] Ibid., 15-16

[4] James D. Whitehead and Evelyn Eaton Whitehead, *Method in Ministry,* 44-45.

significant role here. The Lithuanian Church is not the only Church dealing with this problem in our time.

Future. For the sake of the renewal of the Lithuanian Catholic Church and society, the Church should use the experience of other churches in order to deal with reconciliation more skillfully as well as new studies of reconciliation theology. This would be helpful in today's situation in the Lithuanian Catholic Church.

E. Literature

The literature used in this paper is in three parts: (1) literature on theology and spirituality of reconciliation, (2) study cases of the process of reconciliation world wide, and (3) documents on the Lithuanian Church which will include memoirs of Church dissidents, former underground literature, KGB files and available articles about the Lithuanian Church.

F. Presuppositions

1. The Lithuanian Catholic Church is not a reconciled Church today. There are still priests who belonged to the two opposing factions, those who collaborated or profited from the situation and those who resisted.
2. The former dissidents who are seeking reconciliation have become dissidents again because most of the dissidents oppose reconciliation. And those who are seeking reconciliation are becoming enemies of them, although they suffered together.
3. Those priests, and lay people who collaborated are still in strategic, important positions in the Church, although the details of their collaboration are no longer secret. Wrong doers are quickly trying to forget what happened.
4. What is happening in the Church mirrors the society in general.
5. Even after ten years of independence reconciliation in the Church and societal reconciliation is an extreme need.
6. After the interviews it became clear that reconciliation is more a spirituality than it is a strategy.

G. Limitations

Of course, there are many limitations in this study. First, because of the complexity of the situation, is reconciliation possible? Even if the situation looks hopeless, and, of course, if some the former dissidents will never accept reconciliation, there is no other way of having a future for the Church and for the society than to reconcile. When we are speaking about reconciliation, we mean neither the end of conflict, nor forgiveness, but a process of moral reconstruction of society and the reestablishment of harmony after a time of conflict.

Another limitation is that in this case it is very difficult to distinguish who is a victim and who is a wrongdoer. Limitations and shortcomings aside, social reconciliation in the Church and society is vital. Perhaps this study will be a small contribution to the process of reconciliation as a whole.

CHAPTER ONE:
GENESIS AND PRACTICAL EXPERIENCE

A. How the Soviet Regime Divided the Church

Lithuania was the first Roman Catholic country to come under the Soviet regime. The prelude to the collapse of independent Lithuania was marked by the "period of the three ultimatums" during 1938-1940. In March 1938, while Europe's attention was drawn to the German takeover of Austria, Poland presented Lithuania with an ultimatum demanding the establishment of diplomatic relations, threatening military action in case of refusal. Without foreign support, Lithuania accepted this humiliation. An even more severe shock was the second ultimatum: Germany's abrupt demand in March 1939 that Lithuania cede the Klaipėda Territory. Advised by Britain and France that there was no alternative, the Lithuania government abandoned the country's only major port to the Reich, setting off a domestic political crisis for a government that had always sworn to defend the country's territorial integrity, whatever the odds or consequences. The infamous Nazi - Soviet Pact of August 23, 1939, negotiated by Molotov and Ribbentrop, was another shock to a terrified Europe. This agreement, divided Eastern Europe into "spheres of influence" between Hitler and Stalin, stands as a monument to hypocrisy and cynicism. As part of this *de facto* Soviet-German alliance, the Baltic States (Estonia, Latvia, and Lithuania) were placed in the Soviet "sphere." The pact's immediate effect was to make war inevitable.[1]

The third and final ultimatum, which sealed independent Lithuania's fate, came eight months after the mutual assistance pact with the Soviets. As the Western Alliance reeled from the German offensive in France, the Soviet government accused the Republic of Lithuania of abducting Soviet soldiers and conspiring to create an anti-Soviet military alliance together with Latvia and Estonia. On June 14, 1940, on the same day the Germans entered Paris, the Soviets presented an ultimatum to the

---

[1] *Encyclopedia Lituanica*, s.v. " Soviet-Nazi Pact of 1939."

Lithuanian government demanding, among other things, the admission of the Red Army into the country's population centers. [2]

Even the most optimistically inclined soon realized that Soviet occupation meant more than the end of the president Smetona government and the establishment of a pro-Soviet Lithuanian government. The transitional People's Government headed by leftist journalist Justas Paleckis and some respected Lithuanian democrats had no real power. Lithuanian affairs were directed by Dekanazov, Moscow's plenipotentiary in Kaunas, capital of Lithuania. In mid-July the Communist-controlled security forces carried out the first mass arrests. On July 21, 1940, the ruling diet declared a Soviet Socialist form of government and chose a delegation to proceed to Moscow and "apply" for membership in the USSR, a request granted on August 3, 1940, with the admission of the Lithuanian SSR into the Soviet Union. [3] In that way occupation was completed, but nobody at that time could have predicted what atrocities this regime would bring to Lithuania over the next decades.

The Catholic Church before occupation had strong positions in Lithuania. In 1940, when the Soviet Russians occupied Lithuania, of the more than 3,000,000 inhabitants 85.5 percent were Catholic. Of the remaining, 4.5 percent were Protestant; 7.3 percent, Jewish; and 2.5 percent, Russian Orthodox. The fragmentary 0.2 percent was divided among other faiths. Lithuanians comprised 80.6 percent of the population; 94.4 percent of them were Catholic. [4]

In the two Catholic archdioceses and four dioceses there were 708 churches, 314 chapels, 73 monasteries, and 85 convents, with three archbishops, nine bishops, 1271 diocesan priests, and 580 monks, of whom 168 were priests. The four seminaries had an enrollment of 470. There were also 85 convents, with 950 nuns. [5]

The armed forces, as well as prisons and hospitals had chaplains. There were 18 Catholic primary schools and the same number of Catholic high schools. Religion was taught in all public schools. [6] Atheists and irreligious people were practically non-existent. In 1940 the outlawed Communist party had only 1741 members, of whom, 616 were Lithuanian. [7]

---

[2] Saulius Suziedelis, *The Sword and The Cross* (Huntington, Indiana: Our Sunday Visitor Publishing Division, 1988), 179.
[3] K. V. Tauras, *Guerilla Warfare on the Amber Coast* (New York: Voyages Press, 1962) 16-17.
[4] *Encyclopedia Lituanica*, s.v. "Roman Catholics."
[5] Ibid.
[6] *Encyclopedia Lituanica*, s.v. "Roman Catholics."
[7] J. Savasis, *The War Against God in Lithuania* (New York: Manyland Books, 1966), 13.

B. The First Attack on Religion

Within days of the Soviet invasion, the new government announced its intention to carry out secularization measures, including the abolition of religious instruction in public schools and the end of government support for religious institutions. Since many Lithuanians, including some Catholics, had favored the separation of Church and State and a limited secularization of society, these intentions were not altogether ominous. At first, the government ridiculed any suggestion that it would restrict the practice of religion or the freedom of religious institutions. However, as the regime came under increasingly direct Communist control, and as the Soviets saw less reason to mollify the Catholic masses, the campaign to drive Catholicism from public life escalated. By the end of June 1940, the People's Government had abolished religious instruction in the schools and outlawed religious symbols in public buildings. On July 5 the government formally denounced the concordat with the Vatican and the papal nuncio was ordered to leave the country. On August 15 the regime instituted civil marriage, denied church weddings any legal validity, legalized divorce, and transferred registration of births and deaths to the civil authority. Religious holidays were abolished.[8]

Steadily, the Communists went beyond the secularization of Lithuanian society, undertaking measures clearly aimed at destroying organized Catholicism or restricting it to the practice of a cult without any meaningful social role. On August 28th, *Darbo Lietuva* (*Labor Lithuania*), the official government newspaper, accused the clergy of conducting "anti-people agitation" and warned that "the smell of the Middle Ages" will not be tolerated in Socialist Lithuania. The Church shall not regain its previous position, the newspaper said, and "the clergy must, in good faith, show an understanding for the essential requirements of the new life."[9] On October 2nd, Deputy Commissar of Internal Affairs P. Gladkov, a secret police officer from Moscow, issued an order "to take the clergy into formal accounting."[10] In concrete terms, Gladkov wanted to recruit informers and through them to create dissension among the clergy and also between the clergy and the Catholic population.[11] Secret police began intensively recruiting clergymen, students, and Church servants, though at that time, their efforts apparently yielded negligible results. Three months later, on January 21st, 1941, Commissar of Internal Affairs A. Guzevičius issued another

---

[8] Saulius Suziedelis, *The Sword and the Cross*, 183-85.
[9] *Darbo Lietuva* (Labor Lithuania) (Kaunas) (August 1940): 10.
[10] *Lietuvių Archyvas* (Lithuanian Archive) (Kaunas), Vol. 1 (1942): 28-30.
[11] A. Ž., a.k.a. Spengla V., "LKB Kronikos ištakos, jos balsas Lietuvoje ir pasaulyje," Upublished Manuscript, 6.

instruction. This one requested secret police agencies to take complete inventory of all churches, clergy, and all religious organizations, defunct or yet in existence. The order applied to all denominations. The commissar, furthermore, demanded information about internal conflict, difficulties and needs of individual clergymen. He finally sought more detailed background data about the already recruited clerical and secular informers. Guzevičius acted on orders from Moscow that already was preparing "a plan of available means that operative agencies could use concerning the believers in the newly established Soviet republics." [12] Such actions indicated the government's presumption that the churches were endemically hostile to the regime.

Active police supervision of the clergy generally began only after Lithuania's formal incorporation into the Soviet Union. During the twelve months of Communist rule, some 150 priests, that is, about 10 percent of Lithuania's clergy, were interrogated by the secret police, pressured into spying on their colleagues and parishioners or intimidated to refrain from privately teaching religion. Of these clergy, the NKVD successfully recruited three informers. [13]

Thus, for the Church, the first year of Soviet rule ended on a very pessimistic note. Twenty-four priests were arrested and imprisoned until the beginning of the German-Soviet war; eighteen came out alive. Fifteen additional priests were killed - some tortured - by the withdrawing Communist activists or the military but it was even worse for the country.[14] Early on June 14th, NKVD troops, aided by local Communist officials, began rounding up marked families; they were packed into railroad freight cars for exile from Lithuania. By the time these troops were rudely interrupted on the morning of June 22nd, they had arrested over 17,000 people[15] and shipped them to labor camps in the Altai region, the Novosibirsk and Karelian districts, Kazakhstan and Komi ASSR. Neither expectant mothers nor the sick nor children were exempted from deportation. The ranks of the deportees included members of politically and socially unreliable groups, from Catholic to Socialists, and certain social classes, mainly the more prosperous farmers, businessmen, and community leaders. Clergymen, generally, were spared, and only nine priests were deported.[16] Their turn came in later years.

---

[12] *Lietuvių Archyvas* (Lithuanian Archive) (Kaunas), Vol. 1 (1942):33-34.

[13] Stanley Vardys, *The Catholic Church, Dissent and Nationality in Soviet Lithuania* (New York: Columbia University Press, 1978), 50-51.

[14] J. Savasis, *The War Against God in Lithuania*, 22.

[15] Arvydas Anušauskas, *Lietuvių Tautos Sovietinia Naikinimas 1940 – 1958* (The Soviet Destruction of Lithuanian Nation 1940 – 1958), Vilnius: Vaga, 1996, 137.

[16] Arūnas Streikus,"Lietuvos Katalikų Bažnyčia 1940 – 1990m" in *Metraštis XII*, Lietuvių Katalikų Mokslų Akademija, Vilnius: Katalikų Akademija, 1998, 43.

C. Under Nazi Occupation

In the early morning hours of Sunday, June 22,1941, the Germans attacked the Soviet Union. The Nazi advance was rapid. Lithuania was occupied within a few days. The majority of the local population greeted the war, which was widely understood, as marking the end of Stalinist rule. Initially, the Church hierarchy had welcomed the departure of the communist regime, urging the people to remain calm and carry on under the new administration.[17] The Church managed to partly retrieve its pastoral rights and some of the properties seized by the Communists. Seminaries were re-opened, chaplains returned to their posts in prisons and hospitals, and religious instruction in the schools was again made possible.[18]

The Nazi occupation period, 1941-44, was not an easy one for the Catholic Church. Its schools remained closed. It had no publications. Its property was under the watchful eye of the German occupation authority. In 1942 the Nazis closed the Vilnius Theological Seminary, deported 50 of its seminarians to Germany, and imprisoned about 30 priests. At the same time, they confiscated the convents and forbade the nuns to wear their habits. Thousands of the country's inhabitants were shipped to labor camps in Germany and several thousand, including priests who had given aid to Jews were sent to concentration camps. With the approach of the battle front and the threat of a second Soviet invasion, about 60,000 Lithuanians - among them three bishops and 250 priests - withdrew to Germany.[19]

D. The Second Soviet Occupation

Chaos and violence were the norm in Lithuania during the years that followed the end of World War II. The surrender of Nazi Germany and the advent of Soviets brought no peace, security, freedom, or national independence; in fact, in some districts of Lithuania, the cruel irony was that more Lithuanians met a violent death in the five years following the German surrender than during the entire duration of the Second World War.

In August and September 1945, over sixty thousand civilians were exiled to points east. Between 1946 and 1950, at least a quarter million more of Lithuania's

---

[17] Marian Skabeikis, (ed), *Catholics in Soviet- Occupied Lithuania* (Brooklyn: Lithuanian Catholic Religious Aid, 1981), 25.
[18] Arūnas Streikus,"Lietuvos Katalikų Bažnyčia 1940 – 1990m" in *Metraštis XII*, 42.
[19] J. Savasis, *The War Against God in Lithuania*, 23.

inhabitants were deported,[20] mainly to the Far North, Siberia, and Kazakstan. As in 1941, the exceptionally harsh conditions of the deportations and the difficult situation of the deportees at their destinations meant a high death rate among the victims. The deportations were in large part motivated by the Soviet desire to break resistance to the collectivization of Lithuanian agriculture, a process that was completed by the early fifties.

Perhaps the most violent and traumatic aspect of postwar life was the anti-Soviet partisan war that raged in Lithuania during the mid- and late forties. By early 1945 there were some thirty thousand armed men in the country's forests, although during the eight years of intense warfare (1944-1952) as many as one hundred thousand people may have participated in the anti-Soviet resistance in one way or another. The partisans' ranks were swelled by indiscriminate Soviet repression that made nearly every non-Communist a potential target. At the height of the armed campaign in 1946-1948, the Soviets employed security forces numbering over one hundred thousand men.[21] For a small country, the cost of this "war that followed the war" was frightful: the lowest estimate is that some twenty thousand resistance fighters were killed with at least an equal number of casualties among the occupation forces. Forty thousand partisans where imprisoned.[22] An undetermined but large number of Lithuanian civilians were victims of atrocities carried out by the various Russian and local security units. In addition, thousands of Communist activists and alleged or real pro-Soviet collaborators were assassinated, ambushed, or executed by the partisans. Although out of sight of Western news cameras, the human toll of this conflict was probably greater than the violence that plagued El Salvador during the 1970s and 1980s. More than likely it equaled the agony of Lebanon during the same period. In the end, the lack of any substantive outside assistance and an erosion of popular support due primarily to collectivization ended the main armed rebellion by 1952, although isolated groups of armed men were still reported by the Soviet press in the 1960s.[23]

The fate of the Catholic Church in Lithuania very closely mirrored that of the society at large. At the onset of the second Soviet occupation in 1944 the Communists, still embroiled in war with Germany, officially adopted a conciliatory attitude toward the Catholic Church. During the war atheist propaganda was nonexistent. It is

---

[20] Idzidorius Ignatavičius, *Lietuvos Naikinimas ir Tautos Kova 1940 – 1998* (Vilnius: Vaga, 1999), 575.

[21] A. Ž., a.k.a. Spengla V., "LKB Kronikos ištakos, jos balsas Lietuvoje ir pasaulyje," Upublished Manuscript, 8.

[22] Ibid., 8. See also a very detailed description of Soviet atrocities in Juozas Prunskis, *Lietuva bolševikų okupacijoje* (*Lithuanian Occupied by the Soviet Union*), Chicago: Jūrų Šaulių Kuopa Klaipėda, 1979, 1-240.

[23] Saulius Suziedelis, *The Sword and the Cross*, 195-96.

interesting to note that in November 1944 Nikita Khrushchev, then Ukrainian Communist Party chief, attended the funeral of the popular Archbishop Andrew Sheptytsky of Lvov, the metropolitan of the Greek-Catholic Church, despite the latter's known support for the establishment of an independent Ukrainian state. The Lithuanian Catholic Church also carried out its work with relatively little obstruction during the 1944-1945 period, although the Catholic press, religious education, and the Church's social institutions were not permitted to revive. There was little antireligious propaganda, religious instruction in the parishes was permitted, and three diocesan seminaries with hundreds of students continued their studies.[24]

Even before the Second World War the Soviet machine of propaganda put on their list that the Vatican and the Catholic Church were the number one enemy of the Soviet State. For this reason, the 3rd and 4th decades of the Soviet Union found Catholics being persecuted the most. During that time, the Ukrainian Greek-Catholic Church was liquidated by forcing its merger with the Russian Orthodox. During WWII this policy was even stronger. The Soviets understood that occupied Eastern Europe would face the opposition of a strong Catholic Church. To fight against the Catholic Church, Stalin tried to use the Russian Orthodox Church. Probably this is one of the reasons that the hierarchy of the Russian Orthodox Church met with Stalin on September 4, 1943. As confirmation of this meeting, there is the letter by G. Karpov, the chief of the Council on Religious Affair in Moscow to Stalin in the beginning of 1945. He expressed his opinion to Stalin: "The Russian Orthodox Church can and must play a significant role fighting against the Catholic Church." In May 1945, Polianski, a higher ranking KGB officer, in Moscow issued an order in which he suggested that the head of the KGB in Lithuania promote the Russian Orthodox Church.[25]

The relations between the Communists and the Church worsened after the formal end of hostilities in Europe. Beginning in December of 1945 the Catholic Church was burdened with huge taxes for its buildings and, soon after, churches, monasteries and convents were closed. One of the central problems involved religious education: the terror that intensified throughout the country during 1946 made religious instruction in the churches very difficult, and in 1948 the government banned such activity outright.[26]

From 1944 until the death of Stalin the situation in Lithuania was the same as the current situation in Chechnya. There were strong movements for independence and

---

[24] Ibid., 196-98.
[25] *Lietuvos Vyskupai Kankiniai Sovietiniame Teisme* (Lithuanian Bishops-Martyrs Under Soviet Rule), Vilnius: The Lithuanian Catholic Academy of Science, 2000, 8-9.
[26] Saulius Suziedelis, *The Sword and the Cross*, 195-97.

people continued for ten years to organize partisan war. The KGB tried to use the Church to slow down the partisan movement. They paid a great deal of attention to this matter because the Church at this time possessed a very high level of authority. The first attempt to do this was in 1944. The Soviet official Vitkensas wrote that he succeeded to convince a high-ranking Church official, Prelate Stasys Jokubauskis, that he should write an appeal to the partisans asking them to stop the war. At that time he was administrator of Kaunas archdiocese, because the archbishop and bishop had withdrawn to Germany. Vitkensas got permission from Merkulov, assistant to the director of the KGB, to drive around to the parishes and tell the priests how to announce the appeal in Church. The KGB was very interested in the effect that would have. He did so on June 14, and July 7, 1945.[27] They found that their efforts were useless. The Prelate was condemned by the clergy and by the intelligentsia. Three months later Archbishop of Vilnius Reinys issued a pastoral letter reminding his people of God's commandment "Thou shall not kill."[28] This, however, applied to both antagonistic forces and therefore did not satisfy the communists.[29] It was the first known tension between collaborators – Church administrators and Lithuanian Catholics in the Church hierarchy. They came to the conclusion that the Prelate Jokubauskis was useless. It seems that the KGB killed him, because they did not need a compromised administrator of the archdiocese. It is assumed he was killed because pages 15 and 16 from his KGB file have been torn out.[30]

The KGB tried to convince bishops to collaborate with them. On September 4-6, 1944, an official bishops' conference took place in Ukmergė. They discussed several questions: religious teaching in the schools, establishing a military chaplains' office in the army in which Lithuanians served, and the return of Church property, etc., which showed how naïve they were. The KGB intervened and stopped this conference. Directly from this conference, the Archbishop of Vilnius Reinys was taken to the KGB prison. They kept him for three days. High KGB officials spoke to him trying to force him to collaborate. But they did not succeed. In 1941 eight of his family members were deported to Siberia. The KGB promised to liberate them if he

---

[27] Stanley Vardys, *The Catholic Church, Dissent and Nationality in Soviet Lithuania*, 70.
[28] Vytautas Bagdonavičius (ed), *Arkivyskupas Mečislovas Reinys*. (Chicago: Lietuvių Krikščionių Demokratų Sąjunga, 1977) 189.
[29] *Lietuvos Vyskupai Kankiniai Sovietiniame Teisme* (Lithuanian Bishops Martyrs Under Soviet Rule), 18–19.
[30] *Lietuvos Ypatingasis Archyvas* (The Special Archives of Lithuania - KGB files), Vilnius, file K-1, folder 14, b59, 17-19 (15,16 destroyed). Later: KGB Files.

agreed to collaborate. But the Archbishop did not agree.[31]

They tried to force the bishops to write to the partisans asking them to quit fighting. But the bishops refused. There were two reasons for their refusal: it's a political affair, not a Church affair and if the partisans quit and were captured they would be killed and the Church did not want to accept that responsibility. Second, some bishops were not sure of the prospects for resistance, had a more realistic view of the international situation and did not want to encourage an even stronger resistance and, simultaneously, even more numerous victims. Archbishop Mečislovas Reinys, who for some time before the war had been the minister of foreign affairs and had a good understanding of international affairs, described the international situation in the spring of 1946: "Some people, desiring political changes in our country, expect a forthcoming outbreak of a new war. I find these people very naïve."[32] On February 4, 1946, all the bishops were invited to the KGB office, except Kaosas and Borisevičius who already had been arrested. The commissars of the KGB, the head of religious affairs Polianskis, and other high-ranking officials participated. The main goal was to get the bishops to write an appeal together to the resistance movement. They gave the bishops two weeks. The bishops wrote an appeal but one of the high-ranking Soviet officials interpreted the document and said that if it were printed it would be like a bomb. Then they arrested all the bishops, except the oldest, Paltarokas.[33] The Soviets replaced them by far more loyal Church administrators, the ruling hierarchy of the Lithuanian Church consented to call on the partisans to cease the armed resistance. This attitude did not exert major influence over the slackening of the movement, since the partisans were very well aware of the fact that the statements made by those bishopric proprietors did not represent the genuine voice of the Church.

While striking against the bishops, the Kremlin did not forget the clergy or the rest of the Church. In 1947, the authorities closed all monasteries and convents, dispersed their members and arrested their superiors. Between 1946 and 1948, furthermore, the government proceeded against the middle levels of Church administration, that is, the deans of diocesan districts, and finally, against the more energetic and conspicuous pastors and priests. A total of three hundred fifty-seven clergymen, or one third of all of Lithuania's priests, were arrested and deported.[34]

---

[31] *Lietuvos Vyskupai Kankiniai Sovietiniame Teisme* (Lithuanian Bishops Martyrs Under Soviet Rule), 574-613.

[32] Arvydas Anušauskas, ed., *The Anti-Soviet Resistance in the Baltic States* (Vilnius: Genocide and Resistance Research Center of Lithuania, 1999), 86-87.

[33] A. Ž., a.k.a. Spengla V., "LKB Kronikos ištakos, jos balsas Lietuvoje ir pasaulyje," Upublished Manuscript, 24.

[34] Stanley Vardys, *The Catholic Church, Dissent and Nationality in Soviet Lithuania*, 77.

From this we can see the Soviets' attitude toward the Church. Their goal was to take the leadership of the Church into their own hands. It is very interesting that the head of the Lithuanian SSR Religious Affairs Council, Polianskis, stated in his reports to his superiors in Moscow that he, not the bishops, had been assigning priests to the parishes. The head of the USSR Religious Affairs responded that he should not use that expression because it was politically incorrect. He thought that it was possible to achieve the takeover of leadership and in a more polite way.

The Russian Orthodox Church is different from the Roman Catholic Church. They used a different language, different liturgy, different traditions, and even the Lithuanian and Russian cultures are different. But at the beginning they tried to deal with the Lithuanian Church as they dealt with the Russian Orthodox Church after the October revolution. They tried to separate the Lithuanian Catholic Church from the Vatican. In 1949 the Soviet officials collected signatures on petitions, which asked for the condemnation of the Pope's policies. There was a priest who betrayed partisans, people who fought for Lithuanian independence in the 50's. The Soviets had him in their own plans to use him creating a separate Church from the Vatican. But those plans failed. Even the priests who were at that time KGB agents strongly resisted this policy.

Then the Soviets tried to create Church councils or committees giving lay people leadership in the Church. Their idea was that these committees should be approved by district or city Communist party committees. Of course they thought that by having their own people on those committees they would take the Church leadership into their own hands. Priests would be isolated. They wanted that the priests be left as the "servants of the cult." But they met very strong resistance. Priests, and especially bishops, resisted. The bishops' motivation was that it is a requirement of Canon law that the parish leadership should be in the bishops' hands, and the pastors administrated. There was very strong resistance from the bishops' side. All of the bishops were arrested except the oldest one Paltorokas. Finally in 1948, the Soviets had a little success. But still resistance was strong. Bishop Paltorokas agreed to set up these committees but wanted that the bishop set these up not the government. Finally, after hard and long efforts, those committees were created, but they never had any leadership in the Church during the entire period of occupation. The Soviets kept trying to have the committees lead the parishes. But the priests' authority was well respected and even though the committee was established and registered, all real power was concentrated in the hands of the pastor. In the Russian Orthodox Church they succeeded and that helped to destroy the Russian Orthodox Church greatly. Because when the parish is run by twenty people who are loyal to the government, there are just fights and conflicts. The Russian orthodox ministers were isolated from the leadership. The priests even had to ask the committee for permission to travel outside the parish. They tried to do the same in Lithuania. In the KGB documents instructions required that the government must have one or two agents on these committees.

Later, they had a plan to centralize Church leadership in Lithuania. They thought that it would be easier to control Church people this way. For this reason they had a special KGB case *Apostoli*. They wanted to give the leadership into the hands of one loyal bishop. They tried to do that for seven or eight years but they failed. Then they changed their plan and concentrated Church leadership into three areas, 1) The Archdiocese of Kaunas, Vilkaviškis, and Kaišiadorys had one Church prelate Stankevičius, 2) The Archdiocese of Vilnius and the diocese of Panevėžys were given to Paltarokas, and 3) Telšiai diocese had their own bishop. The KGB put a lot of effort to divide Church administrators and to foster confrontation between them. If they were invited to discuss some issues, they were always invited separately. The KGB had their own agents, informers who reported how Church administrators looked at issues, and used this information to work one prelate against another.

A well-known conflict occurred between the Church administrator Stankevičius and Bishop Paltorokas. There was only one seminary left which was in Kaunas where Stankevičius was the administrator. He felt that he owned this seminary. Paltorokas raised an idea that it is an interdiocesan seminary and the leadership should be collegial. Bishop Paltorokas understood that if the Church leaders would unite their forces it would be easier to resist against the Soviet government. But the Church administrator Stankevičius did not give up until his death in 1957. That year, a Church administrators' conference was held to discuss this issue. After Stalin's death some bishops were released from prison and supported the idea that the leadership of the seminary would be collegial. The bishops' conference signed a protocol but the Church administrator Stankevičius did not sign. This example shows how the KGB used their collaborators to divide the Church. It is known that those bishops who came back from the prisons, especially, Ramanauskas, put a lot of effort into trying to unite the Church administrators, but he did not succeed because the KGB continued to divide the bishops and they had a well-developed network of collaborators among the priests. During this time the KGB failed in creating a Lithuanian national Church but they succeeded in dividing the Church hierarchy and priests as well.

E. Destalinization

Stalin's death rekindled hope, but also created uncertainty about the future. In politics, this uncertainty was generated mainly by the struggle for power in Moscow's Politburo, which at first feigned unity; the leaders apparently feared that an open discord after the loss of Stalin might unbalance the Soviet system itself. In societal relations, ironically, relaxation was promoted by Lavrenti Beria, the dreaded chief of secret police whose power still rested in this notorious institution. Searching for allies in competition for Stalin's succession, Beria eased police pressures and encouraged non-Russian Communist leaders to seek more autonomy for national cadres as well as for national languages. Beria's moves caused many Russians to lose jobs in national republics, and though such personnel policy was restrained after his arrest and liquidation in the summer of 1953, the republics nevertheless were allowed gradually to reabsorb much of their native cultural tradition that Stalin had forced them to eschew. This spirit of tolerance, so aptly named "the thaw" by Ilya Ehrenburg, like a cleansing tide soon spread over the cultural sphere and even religious life, thus producing immense psychological relief for most societal groups.[35]

Stalin's death, and the thaw in the political climate in the USSR immediately following it, brought about new tactics by the Soviets regarding the Catholic Church and the Lithuanian Catholic Church as well, which were timidly begun in the last years of the dictator's life. Their main purpose was to turn the Church into a tool of its foreign policy (like the Russian Orthodox Church or Islam). In order to achieve this, the pressure on the Church and the confrontations with it had to be stopped. The pressure had already weakened by 1950, and in the middle of the 1950s, the regime became relatively more liberal.[36] Unable to establish a national Church, the regime concentrated on appointing reliable Church administrators. They were used for Soviet foreign policy purposes. Thus, in 1951, clergymen were mobilized to sign the Stockholm peace appeal, while Church administrators had to attend Soviet as well as international conferences directed against the American policy in Korea. Four representatives of the Lithuanian church participated in the fourth conference "in defense of peace" that was held in the Russian city of Zagorsk on May 9th-13th, 1952. These four, three Lithuanians and a Polish prelate were prominent Churchmen led by Bishop Paltarokas. Although their speeches, especially those of Paltarokas and Stankevičius, were dignified they invariably paid homage to Stalin, and Paltarokas denounced "the capitalist states" for the alleged use of bacteriological weapons in Korea. Ironically, the Soviet script writers had the quietest of the four, the Very Rev. Petras Maželis, who then administered the diocese of Telšiai, to say the harshest sentences about the United States. Contribution to such propaganda did not end with participation in conferences. After returning home, the bishops and diocesan administrators had to convene a meeting of the clergy for a further discussion of resolutions they brought back, and the clergymen, in turn, had to preach in church,

---

[35] Stanley Vardys, *The Catholic Church, Dissent and Nationality in Soviet Lithuania*, 80-81.
[36] Arvydas Anušauskas (ed), *The Anti-Soviet Resistance in the Baltic States*, 109.

collect signatures for various petitions, and otherwise promote the propaganda of Soviet peace.[37]

Stalin's eventual successor, Nikita Khrushchev, startled the religious community when he stated in November 1954 that there had been excesses in the campaign against the Church. Khrushchev's announcement coincided with a limited relaxation of the Stalinist dictatorship. Thousands of surviving Lithuanian deportees were released from camps or their places of exile as well as the author's family; however, only some were allowed to return to their country. Between 1953 and 1957, about one third (236) of the deported priests and two bishops, Matulionis and Ramanauskas, returned to Lithuania, although the latter was not allowed to resume his episcopal duties.[38]

The Communist Party made other changes. For several years following Stalin's death antireligious propaganda declined. There was even official criticism of primitive and strident atheist indoctrination. In April 1954, *L'Osservatore Romano* reported a radio speech by Bishop Paltarokas outlining some aspects of religious oppression between 1944 and 1953. In 1955 two new bishops, Petras Maželis (he defended Soviet peace very well) and Julijonas Steponavičius, were consecrated and assigned to Telšiai and Vilnius. The new bishops were allowed to visit parishes and administer confirmation, activities that had been restricted for many years.[39]

The tenuous relaxation of tensions between the regime and the Church was also accompanied by a resurgence of faith and confidence among Lithuanian believers. In 1956 the Catholic Church announced that it had received permission to build a new church in the rapidly growing port city of Klaipėda, utilizing donations of the faithful, the first time the Soviet government had authorized such construction. For the first time in over a decade, limited official contact with the Holy See was permitted. Church administrators assigned with the permission of the Soviet government were allowed to travel to the Vatican. Beginning with the late fifties, the regime allowed the publication of a limited quantity of religious literature, mostly liturgical texts and calendars.[40]

The first threatening clouds in Lithuania appeared in 1957. The conflict with the regime was precipitated by Bishop Matulionis, who refused to accept the terms of freedom granted to him. From provincial exile, Matulionis returned to his cathedral to reclaim the position as the Ordinary of Kaišiadorys. On September 25, 1957,

---

[37] Stanley Vardys, The Catholic Church, Dissent and Nationality in Soviet Lithuania, 78-79.
[38] Arūnas Streikus,"Arkivyskupo Teofiliaus Matulionio Santykiai su Sovietine Valdžia 1956 – 1962 m." in *Metraštis XII*, Lietuvių Katalikų Mokslo Akademija, Vilnius: Katalikų Akademija, 1998, 126.
[39] Saulius Suziedelis, *The Sword and the Cross,* 201.
[40] Arūnas Streikus,"Lietuvos Katalikų Bažnyčia 1940 – 1990m" in *Metraštis XII*, 54.

furthermore, he consecrated Rev. Vincentas Sladkevičius as his successor. Matulionis had the Vatican's approval for this consecration, but the government dragged its feet in consenting to the nomination and the old bishop refused to wait any further. The Kremlin now refused to accept the new bishop, and both of them were sent to exile in small villages in Lithuania.[41]

The government's hostility toward the Church further intensified in the early 1960s. The growing enmity resulted from a change in national Soviet policy. Now in complete command of the Party and the government bureaucracies, Khrushchev attempted to apply the brakes to the snowballing emancipation of artistic and intellectual life. He also declared war against the Church and severely tightened controls of all religious activities. In August of 1960, the authorities seized the already completed Church of Mary, Queen of Peace, in Klaipėda. The following year, the government arrested the builder of the church, Rev. Liudas Povilonis, who was its pastor. His assistant, Rev. Burneikis, and five civilians involved in its construction were also imprisoned. In January of 1962, the two priests and the five civilians were brought to trial for stealing state property, black market activities, speculation in foreign currency, abuse of government position, bribery, and charges stemming from alleged violations of the Soviet Republic's criminal code as well as a 1958 national law concerning "state crimes." All were found guilty and sentenced to prison terms from three to eight years.[42] In an arrogant display of callous disregard for people's feelings, Soviet troops, bulldozed the famous Hill of Crosses in 1961.

At the same time, the authorities kept a very watchful eye over the activities of Church administrators and took drastic action in cases of hierarchical noncompliance. Thus, in 1961, the Commission for Religious Affairs was formed. "Cult" members were removed from office and the government banished from Vilnius the administrator of the Vilnius archdiocese, Bishop Julijonas Steponavičius. He was exiled to a small North Lithuanian town for allegedly refusing to ordain two seminarians who were approved by government authorities but whom the leadership of the theological seminary suspected as working for the secret police.[43] The bishop himself did not confirm this explanation, but in 1975, in a letter written to the Chairman of the Council of Ministers of the Lithuanian SSR, Steponavičius indicated that he was dismissed without any stated reasons and merely surmised that he was exiled as punishment for disobeying demands made by the Commissioner for Religious Affairs, Justas Rugienis (1909-1978).[44]

---

[41] Arvydas Anušauskas (ed), The Anti-Soviet Resistance in the Baltic States, 106.
[42] Stanley Vardys, *The Catholic Church, Dissent and Nationality in Soviet Lithuania*, 85-86.
[43] Saulius Suziedelis, *The Sword and the Cross*, 202.
[44] Stanley Vardys, *The Catholic Church, Dissent and Nationality in Soviet Lithuania*, 85.

At the same time, the Soviet government initiated official contacts with the Vatican and thus attempted to "normalize" relations, a process that culminated in 1967 with Soviet President Nikolai Podgorny's visit to the Vatican. The Church also sought an "opening to the East" during the 1960's in the hope of easing the situation of Catholics in Eastern Europe. The Soviet strategy of dealing with the Catholic Church emerged with greater clarity during the 1960's: enforcement of restrictions on religious activity, particularly religious education, while trying to maintain control over the Church administration by allowing the appointment of what the regime hoped would be cooperative bishops. The regime approved the consecration of several new bishops. Juozas Matulaitis-Labukas (1894-1979) was consecrated in Rome in 1965 and was appointed apostolic administrator of the archdiocese of Kaunas. Bishop Juozas Pletkus (1895-1975) was assigned on the same basis to the diocese of Telšiai in 1968, and in the following year Liudvikas Povilonis was designated for Vilkaviškis. Romualdas Krikščiūnas was consecrated bishop and appointed apostolic administrator for Panevėžys.[45] A council of bishops, headed by Matulaitis-Labukas, was formally acknowledged as the governing body of the Lithuanian Catholic Church. During that period of time there was also established another "underground" council of bishops in exile: bishop Julionas Steponavičius, bishop Teofilis Matulionis and bishop Vincentas Sladkevičius. Pope John Paul II named him cardinal during *Perestroika* in recognition of the Church's resistance against the Soviets.

Until Stalin's death the KGB used harsh measures to destroy the Church. Later on they used more sophisticated methods. From a system of violence they came to a more sophisticated method. Of course, during Khrushchev and Brezhnev's times they also used violence. In Khrushchev's days there were many priests who came back from Siberia and after one or two years they were sent back. During Breznhev's times they imprisoned many people, but they tried to avoid publicity.

In all cities and counties Communist party committees had the responsibility of observing how priests in that area obeyed Soviet law. This committee sent their own people to hear what priests were preaching, whether they are saying anti-Soviet things; and if the priest preached against atheistic propaganda it was considered that he was not loyal to the Soviet government. The KGB was also sending its agents and loyal people to listen to what the priests were saying. The Lithuanian SSR Religious Affairs Office was also sending their own to hear what priests were teaching. Because there were so many institutions whose goal it was to persecute the Church, sometimes several state officials listened to the homily of a priest. Then those officials gave a written report, which was part of the case used against the priest to punish him. But

---

[45] Michael Bourdeaux, *Land of Crosses* (Devon: Augustine Publishing Company, 1979), 76-79.

soon they noticed that there were many curious situations. When there was a conflict between the Lithuanian SSR head of religious affairs and the KGB, the head of religious affairs required that loyal priests preach a homily in favor of the Soviets. The KGB was not happy about that because that way their agents could be uncovered. When they finally started to persecute the Church in a more sophisticated way, they began to work more closely together.

They tried to divide the priesthood by these same methods, but with more sophistication. For those priests whom they thought were loyal, they allowed them to fix the churches because many had been damaged during WWII and in that way they created an image among the clergy that the priest was active. And for those who did not collaborate, in most cases, the permission to fix the churches was not granted. Of course, traditional methods were used and fostered the movement of loyal priests to large, important parishes and those not loyal to insignificant parishes.

Every district or city had their own KGB employee whose job it was to keep track of the clergy. For example, in the second biggest city of Kaunas, there was one KGB officer whose job was to watch the clergy, two KGB officers whose job was to watch religious, and at the same time in Kaunas there were 8,000 former political prisoners. The KGB had only two officers to observe these former prisoners. This shows what attention the KGB paid to the clergy. For thirty priests in the town there was one KGB officer. For 8,000 unreliable former prisons there were just two officers.[46]

The KGB used other methods as well. One was a financial method. Those priests who were not loyal had to pay higher taxes. Those who were loyal paid lower taxes. Priests' salaries in a village parish, compared with that of the city parishes, were 10 or more times lower. The KGB paid especially close attention to those who had jobs in the chancery office because those people were in touch with all the clergy. They tried to have as many agents as possible in the chancery office.

One example of this is the case of Rev. Zdebskis who was chemically burned by the KGB when they put a chemical on his car seat in October of 1980. The task was given to some chancery officials by the KGB to spread the story that the priest had two lovers and that what happened to him was revenge.[47] There were many ways in which the KGB divided the priesthood. In one part were the bishops and Church administrators, and in the other part were those who resisted the Soviet regime.

---

[46] KGB files, K-1, folder 14, b 205, 27-30.
[47] See Vidas Spengla. *"Akiplėša," KGB file on Rev. Juozas Zdebskis.* (Vilnius: Lumen, 1996).

F. Emergence of the Dissident Movement

Organized, collective expression of grievances and an articulated defense of vital Catholic interests did not come until 1968. This was the watershed year that marked the beginning of the battle of petitions, arrests, trials, that culminated in the emergence of the underground press, especially *The Chronicle of the Catholic Church of Lithuania*. A search for reasons why the Lithuanian dissents appeared on the scene only in 1968 produces two seemingly contradictory, but actually convergent, explanations. First, while in the late 1950's the hope of improvement in religious conditions was still alive, in the 1960's the prospects of amelioration diminished. In 1961, Khrushchev passed new restrictive Church legislation that first hit the Russian Orthodox and Baptist churches, but that soon affected the Catholics. Two years later, the new restrictions on the clergy were followed by a specially designed atheist campaign that eventually put the local supervision of parish activities in the hands of local atheists. The next year, in 1966, there came the criminal legislation that increased punishment especially for religious teaching and that clearly sought completely to isolate the clergy from society, especially from school age children and teenagers. Thus, the squeeze not only continued, but the "axe" cut much closer to the bone. The Soviets were ready, as the former chief of the Lithuanian Agitprop, P. Misutis, had said, to sever the Church from its future, the youth.[48] The number of priests who disregarded the restrictions on their activities imposed by government, was growing. Between 1961 and 1964, 33 priests were deprived of theirs registration certificates for such violiations.[49]

At the same time, while the party's religious policy turned more reactionary, the general political atmosphere in the country remained several degrees brighter. In the late fifties and the early sixties, Khrushchev attempted to persuade the intellectuals voluntarily to accept the party's supremacy over the arts, but Soviet writers and artists could not be bought off. The permission, in 1962, to publish Alexander Solzhenitsyn's *One Day in the Life of Ivan Denisovich* did not help either. Actually, its appearance in the pages of *Novyi Mir* was an exception to the rule. Censorship, though generally it had been eased, continued to be strict prior to Solzhenitsyn's achievement and remained so afterwards. Already in 1960, many younger writers could not find acceptance in the official press, and this gave birth to literary *samizdat*, a semi-legal private duplication of manuscripts, etc., that the KGB very shortly began to treat as a criminal activity especially after Khrushchev's overthrow in 1964.

---

[48] Stanley Vardys, *The Catholic Church, Dissent and Nationality in Soviet Lithuania*, 128-29.
[49] Arvydas Anušauskas (ed), *The Anti-Soviet Resistance in the Baltic States*, 109-110.

In December of 1965, two Russian Orthodox priests, Nicholas Eshliman and Gleb Yakunin, wrote an open letter to the Patriarch of Moscow accusing him of subservience to the state that hurt the Church.[50]   In April of 1968, to celebrate the international year of human rights that was declared by the United Nations, there appeared *The Chronicle of Current Events*, the chief journal of the Russian dissent movement. In that year Prague Spring took place and the Soviet invasion of Czechoslovakia as well. On April 12th, 1968, the Supreme Soviet of the USSR passed a decree "on the procedure for the examination of proposals, declarations and grievances by the citizens."[51]

All of these developments, the growing suppression especially of religious teaching, the groundswell of demands that raised hopes of reforms, the government's recognition of the right of petition helped to ignite the Lithuanian religious protest movement. They protested anti-Catholic discrimination, the regime's campaign against religious instruction, and even the Catholic hierarchy's passivity in the face of the attack on the Church. The regime reacted harshly to the active clergy's calls for religious freedom, particularly for the freedom of Catholic instruction: between September 1970 and January 1972 four major show trials were held resulting in the imprisonment of clergy and lay persons. The usual response of Soviet authorities to human rights petitions in those years was twofold: official refusal to even acknowledge the appeals, followed by KGB harassment of people sponsoring or signing the petitions.

In March 1972, Lithuanian Catholic dissidents started to print the journal *Lietuvos Katalikų Bažnyčios Kronika* (*The Chronicle of the Lithuanian Catholic Church*, henceforth to be cited simply as *The Chronicle*). It was the first regular underground publication in twenty years since the liquidation of the partisans and their press. The goal of this new Catholic journal, which was at least in part modeled on the Russian dissidents' *Chroinika Tekuschih Sobytij* (*Chronicle of Current Events*), was to report incidents of discrimination against the faithful in Lithuania. It recounts court proceedings against believers and clergy, conflicts within the Church and among the hierarchy, and presents a survey of events concerning religious and Lithuanian national and social life. In this way, *The Chronicle* became a catalyst for mobilizing ideologically diverse sympathies.[52]

---

[50] Stanley Vardys, *The Catholic Church, Dissent and Nationality in Soviet Lithuania*, 131.
[51] Vedomosty Verkhovnogo Soveta Sovetskih Socialisticheshikh Respublik (Moscow), No. 17 (14150), (April 24, 1968): 105.
[52] Saulius Suziedelis, *The Sword and the Cross*, 208- 209.

Historian Saulius Suziedelis, in his book *The Sword and The Cross,* notes:

> One of the *Chronicle's* most attractive features was its philosophy of journalism. It reported only concrete instances of discrimination against believers, avoided excessive rhetoric, acknowledged factual errors on the occasions when they occurred, and cautioned the contributors to provide only credible data. The Chronicle itself was reproduced in limited editions, laboriously retyped or photocopied, then passed from hand to hand until it was smuggled out of the country. However, it was extensively quoted in radio broadcasts to Lithuania, such as those transmitted by Vatican Radio, the Voice of America, and Radio Free Europe: thus *The Chronicle* reached a greater number of people in Lithuanian than would be possible via print alone.[53]

The Chronicle appeared to have two basic purposes. One was to mobilize public opinion at home and abroad, and the second, to provide information and testimony for the Vatican. The Lithuanians dissidents were convinced, as were the Russian dissenters, that especially Western and world opinion could influence domestic Soviet behavior. The editors of *The Chronicle* wrote in 1974: "You cannot expect concessions from the atheists by way of negotiations; The Lithuanian Catholics will have only as much freedom as they will be able to win by struggling for it. The truth of this view has been proven by the several concessions already won in this manner. Lithuanian Catholics however will be capable of making gains only if they will be more widely supported by world opinion and by the high-ranking hierarchy of the Catholic Church."[54]

The Chronicle played a significant role here. Looking at the KGB files we can find that the Soviet officials were very sensitive to world opinion. When *The Chronicle* was broadcast through Vatican Radio, Radio Free Europe and Voice of America, it provoked their reaction. They assigned KGB officers to check on those facts and, of course, KGB officers always found that those facts about Church oppression in Lithuania were wrong. Then the KGB organized their agents to sent letters to Vatican Radio to say that Vatican Radio had aired misinformation. This shows that the Catholic Church and the dissident movement played a significant role during this period of resistance to the Soviet regime.

---

[53] Ibid., 208 – 209.

[54] *Lietuvos Katalikų Bažnyčios Kronika* 2 (The Chronicle of the Catholic Church in Lithuania) (Chicago: Lithuanian Catholic Religious Aid Supporters), No.10 (1972): 122.

At that time the clergy was divided into two parts: dissidents and collaborators or those who profited from this situation. As one former dissident mentioned in his interview, some clergymen became bourgeois during Brezhnev's time. If we talk in terms of percentage, those parts were not equal. For example, the KGB always concentrated their own agents in the bigger cities, strategic places. In some distant counties it was not necessary to have an agent. For example, in the insignificant Joniškis district in 1983 there were no KGB agent priests. Usually, the KGB tried to have at least one.[55] In terms of percentages it was not an equal division. If we talk about those who collaborated with the KGB and those who were loyal to state assigned Church administrators, it was much more than 50%. Those who took an active part in the resistance to atheization and Church oppression were a minority. But they were, as in the Gospel about leavening the leaven, which produced resistance, and they had their own hierarchical support. At that time, there were two bishops in exile from their own dioceses, Sladkevičius and Steponavičius. They were removed from their dioceses and forced to live outside the boundaries of their dioceses in Lithuania. The dissidents, when they needed hierarchal approval, went to these two bishops. For example, *The Chronicle* was approved by the bishops in exile. Even State-assigned Church administrators had to pay attention to the opinion of the bishops in exile because they were removed by the State and the Vatican did not approve of this removal.

When the Soviet officials were pressed for a response, they intensified their foreign propaganda on the "normal" state of Church affairs in the Soviet Union. At home, however, they did not retaliate by drastic administrative measures, but sought instead to contain and minimize the petition's impact on the Lithuanian population. For this purpose the authorities now used the Church hierarchy. A "pastoral" letter was drafted on April 11, 1972, in a meeting with the Lithuanian Commissioner for Religious Affairs Rugienis and Moscow representative Orlov. The clergymen were ordered to read it in all churches on April 30th. It was a broadside against the petitioning priests and their supporters in the parishes. The letter said:

> Order, unity, consensus, mutual trust, trust in our supreme pastor, the Pope, and in individual church pastors remains the essential characteristic of our Church, but some priests and believers hastily and carelessly appraise diverse facts that emerge from the particular moment of history in which the Church lives in our days. Concerned

---

[55] A. Ž., a.k.a. Spengla V., "LKB Kronikos ištakos, jos balsas Lietuvoje ir pasaulyje," Upublished Manuscript, 22.

28

with the individual difficulties that the Church today experiences, some people become pessimistic, draw shortsighted conclusions, begin to distrust even the Providence of God, Christ himself, as if He would not be concerned and would not be taking care of his Spouse the Church. Without any legal right to act, such people take inexcusable actions, as if they were not concerned with the Church's future. [56]

The Church Administrators took this occasion for a criticism of three things. First, the bishops disapproved of parishes that did not accept their appointed pastors but conducted "apostolate" (the letter put the word in quotes) beside and even against their pastor or priest. This obviously referred to the underground Church. Second, the bishops admonished the parishioners not to voice displeasure with clerical transfers because priests were appointed for the "best spiritual advantage" of the believers. Finally, the administrators addressed themselves to the issue at hand:

"In some parishes (they said) irresponsible persons, acting in the name of the clergy and the believers, collect signatures outside of churches, in churches and in private homes on sheets with the text as if of a petition - or even without any text - for the transfer of a priest, not to close a church, to appoint a priest, not to remove the pastor or his assistant, etc. The signature collectors later change or write in their own text and add to it the collected signatures. But this is a falsification. We are very surprised that there are believers who sign without knowing why, what for, and without thinking about the deed's consequence."[57]

This slightly veiled threat of reprisals came out openly in the next sentence:

"We should not forget that the signing of irresponsible writings has an influence on Church relations with the State; that it creates misunderstandings. Such actions cannot bring the Church anything good."[58]

What should they do? The letter contained falsehoods about the collection of signatures - people saw what they signed, and the texts were not changed - but the letter came from Church authorities. As such, it had to be read. But the authorities were widely disobeyed. *The Chronicle* reported " Everyone is very concerned that the Soviet government is increasingly trying to strangle the Catholic Church in Lithuania with the hands of the clergy, …those who had collected signatures and those who had signed demanding freedom of religion in Lithuania were condemned in a "pastoral"

---

[56] Stanley Vardys, *The Catholic Church, Dissent and Nationality in Soviet Lithuania*, 148.
[57] Ibid., 149.
[58] Ibid., 149.

letter." [59] Most of the priests omitted the reading; many read only the religious part that admonished to unity. In its entirety, the letter was read by an insignificant part of the clergy. Nevertheless, it became known in the country because Soviet propagandists continue to quote it as an argument against the "reactionary" priests.

The same year *The Chronicle* printed an article, "The True Situation of the Catholic Church in Lithuania," where the editors wrote: "Everyone is very concerned that the Soviet government is increasingly trying to strangle the Catholic Church in Lithuania with the hands of the clergy and faithful themselves. How is this being accomplished? The Church leadership is being subjugated to the interests of the atheists. Wishing to conceal from the world its treatment of the Catholic Church in Lithuania, and nurturing the hope of deceiving the Vatican in order to obtain there decision favorable to itself, the Soviet government has more than once forced certain Lithuanian bishops and ecclesiastical administrators to publicize to the world incorrect information. For example, the interview of H.E. Bishop J. Labukas published by the newspaper *L'Humanite*; the interview of Monsignor C. Krivaitis, the administrator of the Vilnius Archdiocese, with the ELTA News Agency; the interview granted by H.E. Bishop Pletkus for radio transmission to Lithuanians abroad; and others. In these interviews the following has been maintained: that the present state of the Catholic Church in Lithuania is normal, and that the government is not persecuting the faithful. It is unclear whether the persons referred to really made such statements because many instances are known of interviews being intentionally distorted, altered, and arbitrarily supplemented."[60]

Historian Simas Sužiedelis described the situation in Lithuania at that time in this way: "Catholic and national dissent are closely tied. Like the tsars, the regime knows that by weakening one, it will diminish the other. This is why the Church, as the only remaining non-Soviet national institution, has come under such heavy pressure. Since the Catholic Church is certain to exist in Lithuania for a long time, part of the Soviet strategy has been to undermine its independence and make it a tool of the state. The divisions within the clergy alluded to earlier are, of course, primarily a result of the Soviet presence. This is to say that while each side has accused the other of "destroying the unity of the Church," the sharp differences of opinion between "loyal" clergy and dissident priests have arisen only because of the fact of Soviet rule in Lithuania."[61]

Of course, the most dramatic and public forms of Soviet repression were the

---

[59] *The Chronicle of the Catholic Church in Lithuania* 1 (Chicago: Loyola University Press), No. 4, (1972): 141-43.
[60] *The Chronicle of the Catholic Church in Lithuania*, Vol. 1, No. 4, (1972): 141.
[61] Saulius Suziedelis, *The Sword and the Cross*, 208- 209.

arrests, trials, and imprisonment of both secular and clerical Catholic activists during the seventies and eighties. As it is now known from KGB files, the KGB did all those atrocities. The trials of Fathers Juozas Zdebskis, Prosperas Bubnys, and Juozas Šeškevičius in 1970-1972 were only the beginning. Numerous searches and arrests were carried out in 1973 and 1974. Soviet officials arrested Nijolė Sadūnaitė (born in 1938), Virgilijus Jaugelis (born in 1948), and Petras Plumpa (born in 1948), and many others. One of the most appealing victims of this set of arrests in the mid-seventies was Sister Nijolė Sadūnaitė, who eschewed obvious political motifs and, in her court speech of June 1975, based her entire defense on the principles of Christian charity and support for freedom of expression.[62] She returned from exile in July 1980 but has become even more active than before in defense of religious and national causes.

The interest in the cause of the Catholic dissidents was heightened by the trial in Vilnius of Sergei Kovaliev, the agnostic Russian friend of Sakharov who supported the Lithuanians on human rights grounds and collaborated with the editors of the Lithuanian *Chronicle*. He was removed from the pre-trial investigations in Moscow and it is very likely, as suggested by Sakharov in the Lithuanian *Chronicle*, was sent to the provincial capital of Vilnius to keep him away from friends and to suppress the news of his arrest.[63] Today he is a member of the Russian *Duma*. Among Catholics, the cases that aroused the greatest reaction were the trials of Fathers Sigitas Tamkevičius and Alfonsas Svarinskas, the most active members of the Catholic dissident movement. In May 1983 Svarinskas was sentenced to seven years in prison for preparing "slanderous materials" against the Soviet State. Tamkevičius was arrested at Svarinskas' trial. Thousands of Catholics signed petitions to free them. During that time many were arrested, detained, "informally" harassed, and threatened, but *The Chronicle* continued to appear. The Soviet Government never did succeed in destroying *The Chronicle*.[64]

G. The Vatican and the Dissident Movement

Bishops in exile Julijonas Steponavičius and Vincentas Sladkevičius, who remained popular with the faithful, have been associated with a more determined defense of Catholic rights. They were assigned by Pius XII. Pope Paul VI assigned "loyal" clergy. "Loyalists" naively believe that extensive collaboration with the regime is better for the future of Catholicism, following Vatican "Ostpolitik" under John XXIII and Paul VI. Bishops Liudvikas Povilonis, Romualdas Krikščiūnas,

---

[62] Michael Bourdeaux, *Land of Crosses*, 76-79.
[63] Stanley Vardys, *The Catholic Church, Dissent and Nationality in Soviet Lithuania*, 192–193.
[64] Ibid., 227-28.

Juozas Pletkus, Monsignors Krivaitis and Gutauskas, the administrators of the archdiocese of Vilnius, adopted "loyal" positions. Pope John Paul II added a few more "loyal" bishops, Antanas Vaičius, Juozas Preikšas and Vaclovas Michelevičius.[65] From the view point of Communist countries the new political policy of Pope Paul VI had success in those countries where the religious persecution was not so severe, namely, Poland, Eastern Germany, and Hungary. Where the communist regime persecuted the faithful very severely, namely, Czechoslovakia, Albania and the Soviet Union including Lithuania, this political policy brought no benefit. As for Lithuania, the policy perhaps resulted in even greater confusion.

The dissident movement message to the Vatican was similarly clear. *The Chronicle* has disapproved "certain unfavorable decisions"[66] the Vatican has made in the past, has criticized the silence Rome had kept about the persecution in Lithuania, and has objected to Vatican concessions that made it easier for the Commissioner for Religious Affairs to interfere in clerical appointments. *The Chronicle*, furthermore, opposed favors granted to "loyal" priests and disapproved of certain episcopal and administrative appointments because of their considered harmfulness to the Church.

The basic message that *The Chronicle* stressed again and again was the conviction that "the Soviet government has intensified the drive to strangle the Lithuanian Catholic Church with the hands of our own clergymen and believers."[67] In other words, the Kremlin was trying to destroy the Church from within. Lithuanian Catholics, *The Chronicle* said, even risked the publication of a clandestine journal to warn the Vatican that it is not persecution, but the self-tied hangman's rope, that presented the greatest danger to the Church. *The Chronicle* further complained that clergymen who actually work for the secret police are frequently considered as people "who know how to adapt to conditions of persecution." "Such priests try to justify themselves by claiming that they are not destroying the Church but merely seeking "dialogue" with the Soviet government. The Vatican, it appears, does not understand what this "dialogue" means. It is a total capitulation, the complete betrayal of the Church cause."[68]

In spite of condemning the dialogue furthered and directed by government-controlled administrators, *The Chronicle* did not oppose Vatican communications with the Communists *per se*. After the Soviets Foreign minister Gromyko's visit to the Vatican in 1974 *The Chronicle* wrote, "The Catholics are convinced of the necessity of a dialogue, but without illusions. It can be useful if good will is displayed on both

---

[65] Marian Skabeikis (ed)., *Catholics in Soviet- Occupied Lithuania*, 49-60.
[66] *The Chronicle of the Catholic Church in Lithuania*, Vol. 1, No. 4. (1972): 147.
[67] Ibid., 141.
[68] Ibid.

sides... Up to the present time the Communist regime, in the view of the Catholic faithful, uses only deceit and force. It appears that, for the regime, dialogue with the Church is only needed so that the Vatican, hoping that the conditions of the faithful would be lightened, would be silent about the persecution of Catholics in the Soviet Union. The dialogue serves to have the world hold the false opinion that religious freedom exists in the Soviet Union."[69] It was wrong, however, editors of *The Chronicle* believed, to assume the existence of such an attitude on the Communist side.

The Chronicle finally criticized the perceived Vatican prescription for the solution of Lithuanian problems. The Roman Curia, the publication suggested, thought it possible to normalize the situation by reestablishing Church organization, concretely, by appointing more bishops and then by adopting an appeasing stand toward the Soviet government. In Lithuania's situation, however, the number of bishops was sufficient "and new appointments are not wanted."[70] *The Chronicle* again underlined this conviction seven years later, in its distress signal of October 1979:

"Frequently rumors are heard that new bishops will be named in Lithuania. This is understandable since both the Lithuanian clergy and the Holy See wish to normalize the affairs of the Lithuanian Church. *The Chronicle* is convinced, however, that there is very little hope of achieving this. The Soviet government would not allow the Lithuanian Church to reap any benefit from the appointment of a new bishop, and the faithful would accept only bishops who were not government collaborators and who would not capitulate in the face of danger."[71]

In an address to Cardinal Bengsch of East Berlin, who visited Lithuania on August 22-26, 1975, *The Chronicle* criticized the alleged Vatican advice to Lithuanian Catholics not to engage in conflict with Soviet authorities:

"We do not know whether this really is the advice of the Holy See, but if this principle for relations with the Soviet government would prevail, we would need to abandon essential pastoral duties, for example, the catechization of children. This would create a source of continuous conflict with our conscience. We would then become real "servants of the cult," as the Soviet government wants to have it."[72]

At the same time, the editors predicted the consequences of the Vatican policy:

---

[69] *Lietuvos Katalikų Bažnyčios Kronika* (The Chronicle of the Catholic Church in Lithuania), Vol. 2, No. 9. (1974): 78.

[70] *Lietuvos Katalikų Bažnyčios Kronika* (The Chronicle of the Catholic Church in Lithuania), Vol. 2, No. 10 (1974): 115.

[71] *The Chronicle of the Catholic Church in Lithuania*, Chicago: The Society of the Chronicle of Lithuania, Vol. 6, No. 40 (1979): 8.

[72] *Lietuvos Katalikų Bažnyčios Kronika* (The Chronicle of the Catholic Church in Lithuania), Chicago, Lithuanian Catholic Religious Aid Supporters, Vol. 3, No. 19, (1975): 177-178.

Because of the persecution of the faith [they said], pastoral work is already partially conducted in the conditions of the catacombs, and the Soviet government, with good reason, is afraid of underground work because it cannot control it. The more the government restricts official Church activities, the more intensive becomes the secretly conducted pastoral work. Government-inspired priests attempt to picture this work as harmful and destructive of Church unity as well as of normal Church-state relations. However, if at this time the Catholic Church in Lithuania would not adapt itself to the underground work conditions, she would be threatened by the fate of the Russian Orthodox Church; this Church has been almost completely smothered.[73]

The Chronicle kept repeating this warning during the entire year of 1977: "one gets the impression that in order not to spoil relations with Moscow's atheists, (world) Catholics have chosen the tactics of silence. The Holy Father is supposed to have said 'It is necessary to pray and to wait quietly and with patience.' We are accustomed to being deceived, and we do not believe that the Holy Father would so have advised us." The duty of the Church, the editorial further pointed out, is to evangelize. How can this duty be reconciled with silence? " How can we keep silent and wait when the atheists neither stay silent nor wait?"[74]

From the early 80's *The Chronicle* tried not to criticize Vatican politics directly. A formula of survival was found. From one side the Vatican did not want the Catholic Church in Lithuania to become a totally underground Church. From the other side, they tried to support an underground Church movement. Vatican officials from one side said there was a need to seek dialogue with the Soviet government and for as much as possible to act legally. From the other side, the Vatican supported the underground Church, especially morally. For example, Vatican Radio always broadcast articles from *The Chronicle*. In that way it can be said that Vatican politics under Pope John Paul II were realistic. They dealt with the Soviet State supported hierarchy and Church administrators and also quietly supported the underground Church movement. Without the underground Church in these circumstances, it would be very hard to resist against the Soviet regime. The Underground Church movement

---

[73] *Lietuvos Katalikų Bažnyčios Kronika* (The Chronicle of the Catholic Church in Lithuania), Chicago: Lithuanian Catholic Religious Aid Supporters, Vol. 3, No. 17 (1975): 8.
[74] *The Chronicle of the Catholic Church in Lithuania*, New York: Lithuanian R.C. Priests' League of America, No. 28 (1978): 13.

indirectly helped Church administrators to resist Soviet pressure. During the last decade of the dissident movement, the Vatican politic was not criticized directly, but the Church administrators and priest who were "loyal" to the Soviet regime were criticized up to the last year of the persecution. In October of 1984 the editors of *The Chronicle* wrote:

"The Apostolic See has condemned the efforts of atheists to destroy the Church in Nicaragua. For a long time the atheists have been trying to do the same in Lithuania by various attempts to promote clergy disloyal to the Church to influential hierarchical Church positions. Almost exclusively through such clergy does the government allow official information to be given to the Vatican. Up to now only a minority of priests have submitted to government pressure. So government security forces are putting forth enormous efforts to make those yielding to government pressure the majority in the future."[75]

A Lithuanian American and Professor of Political Science at The University of Oklahoma Stanley Vardys in 1978 noted: "The journal's language was somewhat more direct than the Russian Chronicle; sometimes it was sarcastic and angry."[76] *The Chronicle* remained faithful to this style till the end. Even when Gorbachov gave a little religious freedom, editors of *The Chronicle* in 1987 wrote:

"Consequently, atheism, realizing that it cannot overcome the defenders of the Church directly, has long ago resorted to use the means used by all totalitarian powers, namely, "Divide and Conquer." One of the schemes is an invitation to "unity" (a peculiar paradox!) so that through the efforts of some Catholic Church leaders or clergy there would be a breakdown of opposition to violence, persecution, and government control of the Church, on the part of fervent and loyal defenders of the faith. That's why there was a whole list of benefits promised to those who stood for " unity:" better, more prosperous parishes, proper titles, even episcopal positions."[77]

H. Personal Experience During the Times of Persecution

I was involved in Church activities when I was in school in 1973. I was also an altar boy in the diocesan cathedral. Two years later I already belonged to the underground organization known as Brothers of the Holy Eucharist, which was a youth organization, lead by those opposed to the Soviet regime. It did not take long for

---

[75] *Lietuvos Katalikų Bažnyčios Kronika* (Chronicle of the Catholic Church in Lithuania), Chicago: The Society of the Chronicle of Lithuania, Vol. 8, No. 64, (1984): 218.

[76] Stanley Vardys, *The Catholic Church, Dissent and Nationality in Soviet Lithuania*, 156.

[77] *Lietuvos Katalikų Bažnyčios Kronika* (Chronicle of the Catholic Church in Lithuania), Chicago: The Society of the Chronicle of Lithuania, Vol. 8, No. 73 (1987): 320.

me to discover that our Church was divided. The bishop and a few priests in the cathedral were defending "peace," as the Soviet regime wanted which required that many compromises be made with the Soviets. During the meetings of the Brothers of the Holy Eucharist, the leaders expressed different ideas, as they opposed any kind of collaboration with the Soviet regime. During these meetings, they tried to show us how unjust the Soviet system was and to build in the hearts of young people a love for the Church and the people of Lithuania. It was very clear that the Church was divided when the leaders of the Holy Eucharist organization warned us not to talk about our meetings with certain priests. All these meetings were held secretly. First, it seemed strange to hear the warning of not talking to some of the priests, but now that the codenames of the KGB for these priests are known it is very clear why these warnings were made. In 1981 the KGB officer from Panevėžys wrote a report to the head of the KGB headquarters in Vilnius. "There are no extremist priests in our territory. But, we have separate "servants of the cult," especially among the young ones, and they are influenced by reactionary priests. They are trying to widely spread ideologically damaging ideas. Those priests are Banulis and Pukenis. We have five priests who were sentenced for crimes against the state (the KGB officer had in mind those sentenced during Stalin's time). Right now they are in a respectful age, and we do not have information about their activities against the state. Under the leadership of the religious element (KGB officer had in mind nuns), in our days we are noticing that *Bičiuliai* (Brothers of the Holy Eucharist) were trying to more actively spread their activities. They are organizing religious pilgrimages to shrines. They are organizing gatherings. They are trying to involve more young people. There are about one hundred members who belong to this group in our city."[78] I learned very early the Church was divided in two parts- those who decided to collaborate and those who did not.

I did not experience KGB persecution while I was in high school and served as altar boy in the cathedral. As I learned later the reason why they did not persecuted us was they needed altar boys for "peace" shows in the Cathedrals. Altar boys in small towns at that time were hardly tolerated. I saw Cardinal Bengsch of East Berlin, who visited Lithuania in August 1975. This visit for an eleven-years-old altar boy was very impressive. The editors of *The Chronicle*, as I now learned, had a totally different opinion. *The Chronicle* cautioned Cardinal Bengsch: "We believe that by its diplomatic activity the Holy See sincerely wants to help the persecuted Church. However, because of the lack of knowledge of concrete circumstances, in some situations the Holy See may find itself helping the interests of only the atheists. We therefore dare to warn you: do not believe the promises of the Soviet government

---

[78] KGB Files. K–1. Ap. 14. B. 621. 66-67.

36

because they will not be fulfilled. Do not believe those who officially come from the Soviet Union - all of them more or less are obliged to execute the assignments of the party and the KGB."[79]

In October of 1979, the Hungarian Cardinal Lekai arrived at our cathedral, where a large crowd of believers awaited. The cathedral bells rang, the crowd sang, and girls stationed the length of the cathedral covered the cardinal's path with flowers. It was an impressive ceremony for an altar boy, but *The Chronicle* was not happy about this visit: "It is a great pity, however, that the Ordinaries of Lithuania do not have the right to freely invite members of the Church hierarchy of their choosing but must be contented with those whom the Soviet government designates. After all, Cardinal Lekai came at the invitation of Moscow and the Patriarch of all Russia, Pimen, and not at the request of the Lithuanian Ordinaries. If the Soviet regime permitted, perhaps even advised, the Patriarch to invite a Catholic cardinal, it did so only with the hope of gaining from the visit considerable benefits for themselves. It is difficult to believe that its hopes were fulfilled."[80]

Now I would like to explore two cases about my direct experience with the KGB. When two famous dissidents Rev. Alfonsas Svarinskas and Rev. Sigitas Tamkevičius were arrested in 1983, I was studying at the Kaunas Technological University and belonged to the *Bičuliai* group in the city. We decided to collect signatures on a petition asking the Soviet authorities to free these two priests. We went to a small town, Vievis, whose parish held a Lenten retreat. Two young women students and I collected signatures during all the Masses. Almost everybody signed. Then we noticed that the KGB had surrounded the Church. All petitions were left in the Church's confessional. The young women mixed with the crowd and managed to escape unnoticed. I was not so fortunate. I was caught by the KGB officers and arrested. I was interrogated for 12 hours. They tried to convince me that I was committing a crime collecting signatures, but they had no evidence that I had committed this crime. Then they freed me; and after a few interviews at my university, one of the KGB officers said to me that the Red Army would correct me.

After three months, I was sent to the Red Army where I experienced only one incident when they found a rosary in my pocket. Because of the Orthodox tradition in Russia, they did not understand what the rosary was. After some arguments that it was a family relic, it was given back to me. Of course, religious symbols in the Red Army

---

[79] *Chronicle of the Catholic Church in Lithuania*, New York: Lithuanian R.C. Priests' League of America, No. 19 (1978): 12.
[80] *The Chronicle of the Catholic Church in Lithuania*, Chicago: The Society of the Chronicle of Lithuania, Vol. 6, No. 40 (1979): 3-4.

were forbidden.

The third arrest followed soon after I was released from the Red Army. With two friends I went to Žemaičių Kalvarija, our national shrine, during a feast day when many people travel to the shrine. I stayed at the shrine overnight. When I was leaving early the next morning to the church, the police caught me. They were suspicious about my sleeping bag. They thought that I was smuggling religious items. But, when the police found only a sleeping bag and some food, they said it was okay. But, they said that I would have to go to the second floor, which is where the KGB had set up their offices during the religious festival in this town. There, I had a conversation with a young KGB officer whose name was Raimondas. He asked where I was studying and what I was doing. I told him that I was just back from the Red Army and that I was a student at the Kaunas Technological University. Two weeks before this interrogation I had filed my application for the Kaunas Seminary, but I did not mentioned this fact to the KGB officer. Then he asked me why I was here at a national shrine, that after the Red Army one should go to a resort and have fun. I explained that it was my way of belief. Then he started to talk. He said that the KGB was a very strong organization, and that it made great sense to belong to this organization. He gave me his personal example. He told that he finished the Technological University in Vilnius as well, but his salary was very low. Then he changed his profession. He became a KGB officer, and he had a salary four times higher than previously. He tried to be very friendly to me and gave me a suggestion. "Look, Rimantas," he said, " when you finish university and become an engineer, and your salary will be very low. I have for you a different suggestion. Because right after the Red Army you are not going to resorts to have fun with girls, you must change your school. You have to enter the seminary and to become a priest. For you to enter it would be very easy because we will help with the exams. You know that we control this place (the seminary). You know that priests make more money than engineers. Of course, we will help you as well financially."[81] I said that everything for me was very sudden and that I would have to think about it. Then he told me, "Okay, go to the shrine and pray, observe, maybe someone will be distributing illegal literature. And then let us meet together after a few hours; and you will report to me what you found and maybe you will like our agreement."[82] When he dismissed me, I immediately left town.

In this way, I experienced how the KGB was trying to divide the Church and in what cynical ways they were trying to make their own agents. Soon after that I had another invitation to have a meeting with a KGB agent. All candidates who applied for seminary were interview by the KGB. I was instructed by the priests from the

---

[81] KGB Officer Raimondas, interrogation of the author, 2 July 1985.
[82] Ibid., 2 July 1985.

resistance movement how to behave in these situations. Because they were trying to destroy the Church from within, they allowed only those who were weak, not very intelligent, young men to enter the seminary. And if they found that this young man has agreed to work for them for money, he would be a good candidate. During this interview the KGB officer asked me to sign and not to tell anyone that I had agreed to collaborate. I told him that I would have to think about that because after the Red Army I had some emotional problems, and that I had started talking in my sleep. Being in a seminary, when I would have to sleep in the same room as my classmates, I could betray our deal during the night. Then he asked why I was entering the seminary. I gave three reasons: 1) I like to fix churches; 2) I like to have more free time and to read books; and 3) I like to have lots of money and to travel around the Soviet Union. I said this because of the instruction I had received in terms of what to say and what not to say. The KGB liked not very intelligent, greedy, and lazy candidates. Then he set another appointment with me for one month later for me to think and to sign the collaboration documents. Within this month I received the confirmation that I was accepted in the seminary, and I did not show up for my appointment.

When I entered the seminary, the division was very clear. The seminarians who came with the protection of the KGB or recommendation of the KGB collaborating pastors were different from the seminarians who had decided not to collaborate. Most of those seminarians who opposed the idea of collaboration belonged to underground religious communities, Franciscans and Jesuits. I joined the underground Jesuit community. *The Chronicle* at that time wrote about the seminary: "That civil authorities should not interfere with the administration of Kaunas seminary for the priesthood, particularly in the selection of administrators, teachers, and even seminarians. Since normal conditions did not prevail, there is a great deal of evidence that ordinations to the priesthood are conferred on some who are not interested in the spiritual welfare of the faithful and who have no desire to live it themselves. This not only saddens but also harms the Church. The sad fact is that some who suffer psychological illness have been ordained too."[83] Some Catholic dissidents have gone so far as to suggest that ninety percent of the student body at the seminary has been infiltrated and that the Church would be better served if the school were closed.[84]

Now that the KGB files have been unsealed, we know that in 1982, of 92 seminarians, 18 were agents. Of these 18, only 9 had collaborated voluntarily. There was one special agent "Žilvinas," who had a salary. In 1985, there were 27 KGB

---

[83] *Lietuvos Katalikų Bažnyčios Kronika* (Chronicle of the Catholic Church in Lithuania), Chicago: The Society of the Chronicle of Lithuania, Vol. 9, No. 70 (1986): 129.
[84] Saulius Suziedelis, *The Sword and the Cross*, 225.

agents out of 100 and 60% of the professors in the seminary were KGB agents. [85] In 1988, KGB General Eismuntas issued directives that heads of city and district KGB offices should recruit for the seminary men who do not believe in God because they were not satisfied with the agents who believed in God. It was a practice from Russia where the KGB tried to destroy the Russian Orthodox Church. The general in his letter writing said that the seminarians who believe in God when they completed the seminary in many cases refused to collaborate. Some of them even made public statements that the KGB forced them to collaborate. Probably he had in mind the Rev. Puzinas' case. Because of this, he thought that the best way would be to have non-believers enter the seminary. It is interesting to note that these plans were put in effect in 1988 when Cardinal Sladkevičius allowed everyone to enter the seminary, even those who were opposed by the Soviet regime. But the KGB had a different vision of the Church even during the time of *Perestroika*.

First of all, the KGB did not expect that *Perestroika* would cause the collapse of the Soviet Empire. From studies of KGB officers' notes and from files, it can be determined that they had a different idea about what would happen. But most of them demanded that *Perestroika* be stopped. They were not happy with *Perestroika*. Just some of the KGB agents supported *Perestroika*. The official KGB position was to promote but to control *Perestroika* according to the guidelines of the Communist Party Central Committee. Of course, they were planning to continue to have control of the Church. But new social situations required new methods. During *Perestroika* there was more freedom and more possibilities to travel, even for those who resisted the Soviet regime. In this situation, the KGB organized a new case, so called "Capella." Through the network of their agents they tried to convince the Vatican that the Church would get more freedom if they would have a dialogue with the Soviet government. KGB agents going to the Vatican popularized that idea. From the other side, through the network of their agents, they tried to influence Vatican politics. For example, during *Perestroika* they understood that they would not win the war in Afghanistan. They were looking for a strategy to escape from this situation while saving face. So the KGB forced their own agents in conversations with Vatican officials to define the war in Afghanistan as a fight for peace. In this situation, we can see that there was a shift in KGB methods. They were using their own agents not only for spying but also to influence.

Perestroika came very slowly to the Lithuanian Catholic Church. First it was when *Sajūdis*, the Lithuanian Movement for *Perestroika*, was created in 1988. The

---

[85] A. Ž., a.k.a. Spengla V., "LKB Kronikos ištakos, jos balsas Lietuvoje ir pasaulyje," Upublished Manuscript, 12.

Lithuanian Catholic Church quietly supported *Sąjūdis*. The Church did not play a significant role in the *Sąjūdis* movement. The hard-headed official in charge of religious affairs was removed. When the bishop in exile Sladkevičius became a cardinal in 1988, he ignored the Soviet rule that all candidates to the seminary must be approved by the Soviet regime. He allowed all men to enter who wished to enter, and he removed those he did not trust. One wrongdoer was removed from a high position in the seminary administration the same year. Soon the Vatican took a step without consulting with the Soviet officials. They made Cardinal Sladkevičius the head of the Lithuanian Bishops' Conference.

This case from my personal experience will help to understand why *Perestroika* came to the Church slowly. Being in the underground youth movement Brothers of the Holy Eucharist, I met many wonderful people. One priest at that time impressed me deeply. I shall call him Father John. He was an effective leader of young people. Father John's speeches were deep, and easy for young people to understand. He was a wonderful spiritual director for my friends and me. He was also a patriot supporting Lithuanian Independence. He helped us to understand the danger of Soviet propaganda and the importance of knowing our national heritage. He taught us to love Jesus and our faith. Because the documents of Vatican II were not available he taught the faith from a pre-Vatican II perspective.

He was a famous dissident and persecuted by the Soviet regime. The government never allowed him to be assigned to a parish. This served him well because he had more time for his underground activities: fighting against the Soviet regime, he did a lot, and at the same time had to be very careful; trusting just a few reliable people. He did a lot for our nation during this time. He was a model for me personally. As a spiritual director, he showed others and us the important values of freedom, human rights, and faith.

The independence movement *Perestroika* started. Soon the Soviet Union collapsed and Lithuania became a free country. There were many changes in Lithuanian society at that time. Many people welcomed liberty, democracy, and the freedom to practice their faith, yet some people found this new way very difficult. Even some priests found it very difficult to accept all the changes. It was a doubly difficult time for the Church and its people, because they had to accept all the new changes in their democratic society, and in the same way they had to start to live the spirit of Vatican II.

During Soviet times, it was impossible to reform the Church because the government controlled the Church. After a few years of independence, the situation changed dramatically. The circumstances in the social, political, educational, and ecclesiastical spheres evolved from dominant authority imposed from above, to sharing in authority.

Father John found these changes very difficult. He started to lose his popularity in society and in the responsibilities to which he was assigned. There were several reasons for this: First, he did not accept changes, which were taking place in society and in the post Vatican II Church. He could not adapt to the new ways of behavior in the new society. Second, during the long years of the Soviet regime, he became accustomed to fighting the government. When freedom came, he was so accustomed to fighting the government that he continued to be suspicious, and he was always looking for someone with whom to fight. The object of his anger was the changes, which were taking place in the new Church. He was preaching that all the changes were bad and had been brought from the West. There were dramatic differences in our relationship as compared to the time of my youth. During those days, I admired him because he was a strong leader in the resistance movement. But at this time we had many arguments about how to accomplish our tasks in the ministry.

Mixed feelings developed because in one situation Father John was my life model and when democracy came to Lithuania, he was an example of how not to be. Thinking and studying about why this was happening, I found that for many dissidents and resistance leaders, this new period of freedom was very difficult. They were unable to adapt easily to a new situation. Their actions were built upon a strategy of resistance. They concentrated so much on the idea of resisting and on relying on a limited, trusted group of people that they could not adapt to the changes introduced by anyone but themselves. They were suspicious of every change because during Soviet times every change from the government brought bad things- imprisonment, persecution, etc.

My first assignment as a pastor revealed those difficulties even clearer. I became a pastor for the first time, two and a half years after my ordination in 1992. The reason that I was assigned as a pastor so early was the Jesuits of Lithuania had a dream to rebuild the Jesuit province in the same way that it existed before communism. Klaipėda, which is a big seaport city, was totally destroyed near the end of WWII when the Russian troops were pushing the German troops back to Germany. All churches were bombed and destroyed in the city. During Soviet times there was one small worship space, which could contain 200 people. When I became the pastor, there were 250,000 people in Klaipėda; and in the territory of my parish, there were 80,000 people. It was a multi-cultural parish that included Lithuanians, Russians, Belorussians, Poles, and Ukrainians. People in the parish were very atheized. Sunday attendance was 1,000, and on Christmas, there were 6,000 in attendance.

At the time, I was a newly ordained priest and a Jesuit novice. My friends called me "Pastor Novice." The reason this happened was that the Jesuit provincial wanted to restore all Jesuit activities to pre-Soviet Lithuania levels. He did not pay attention to the fact that not every Jesuit who lived in oppressed times and was advanced in age were capable of acting in new ways for the renewal of the Church nor management of parish affairs. The Jesuits were severely oppressed by the Soviets. They were allowed to work in tiny parishes in Lithuania and they became accustomed to acting alone and living alone. Community life was foreign and difficult for them.

I came to this parish immediately after my studies at the University of Illinois at Chicago and after one year of experiencing Jesuit life with the Jesuits who taught at St. Ignatius Preparatory School in Chicago. It was an experience, which taught me what "post-Christendom" community means. When I went back to Lithuania, it seems like I stepped back a few centuries into a Jesuit Christendom community.

To be a pastor in a parish was a challenging responsibility for me. I think I was successful in developing parish committees to mobilize the community to do charitable work, to develop ministries, etc. During that year, seven or eight young men entered the seminary. It was interesting and fun to work with people. But when things came to community life and my associate pastors, my life became complicated. The older associates thought that I was young and dumb, without experience, and doing everything wrong. When things went wrong in the parish, everyone remembered that I was the pastor and reminded me that I was responsible. When I wanted to demonstrate my leadership to my associates, they were very quick to remind me that I was just a novice. After a year of that leadership, I left the Jesuits and moved to the diocese where I was born and ordained. I wrote a letter to Father General Kolvenbach and I want to cite part of this letter, which demonstrates my "leadership" situation.

Dear Father General:
Allow me to begin this letter with a brief introduction. I was ordained a priest for the Diocese of Panevėžys, Lithuania, on May 27, 1990. From July 7, 1989, until January of this year I was a novice in the Society of Jesus. In the letter dated January 7, 1993, Lithuanian Provincial, Father Boruta, informed me that I had been dismissed from the Jesuits. I have great respect for the Jesuits and owe very much to them. My hope had been to give my life to God as a Jesuit. My closest and best friends remain Lithuanian Jesuits…

Let me explain the difficult situation in which I found myself in Klaipėda. When I went to Klaipėda, Father Baliūnas was the pastor and I was an assistant. There was a major building program in its early stages, a very large church was under construction. I understood, Father Baliūnas was not the priest to lead the parish at that time, and I was named pastor because of the organizational and leadership abilities I had shown. As pastor I went to work not only with the building program but also organizing youth, etc. I had two assistants, Father Šeškevičius and Father Jonas Zubrus, who were seventy-eight years and sixty-nine years of age respectively. I was twenty-eight years old and a novice. Both had been pastors in village parishes in

43

Lithuania and other parts of the Soviet Union throughout the communist years. Father Šeškevičius was three times tried, convicted, and imprisoned by the Soviets. They were both good priests and most dedicated to the Church.

A very serious difficulty developed when as pastor I would communicate parish plans and programs to the people in the parish. Then Father Šeškevičius would go to the pulpit after I went to the sacristy and tell the people not to pay attention to what I said and tell them other plans. Some of this related to the new church under construction. I was proposing, with the bishop's approval, to modify the church plans to be more in conformity with Vatican II liturgy and to be more within the parish budget.

I did not mention all the problems to the Father General though there were many. For example, to get permission to change the church project was not easy. But, a famous Lithuania architect V. K. Jonynas helped a great deal. All his life he had lived in the United States, where he had designed about 50 churches. When Pope Paul VI visited New York City, Jonynas designed the liturgical worship space. Using his authority I convinced the Bishop and my provincial that the church project needed to be changed. Jonynas told that this building was a post-socialist monster with the tallest towers in the country. It contained the biggest worship space as well. It was hard to convince the Bishop and the provincial, but it was impossible to convince my associates. When the changes were approved and the architects began working on the new plans, one of my associates was preaching from the pulpit that, "Catholic Lithuanians resist. Our pastor wants to change the church project. After his changes, the church will not look like a Catholic church but like a sect church. We defended against the Czar's regime the Kražai Church. We will defend this church."

The Kražai affair is a story of the resistance of the Lithuanian Church against the Czar's regime in 19th century. Even though the church was closed, after this massacre the Czar was hesitant to close other churches. As I understand currently, my associates engaged in a theology of resistance even when we lived in an independent country. They managed again to convince the bishop and my provincial not to change the original plan. At this time our inflation was very high, and people were so poor that the Sunday collection would not even be able to pay to heat the church building.

The theology of resistance was met in every change. We had a temporary church, which was not big enough to hold the parishioners on Sundays, even if they stood. According to the spirit of Vatican II, I decided that communion should be accepted standing. Then my associate preached that we should not let the pastor destroy our faith, that in Žemaičių Kalvarija, we did not allow the Soviets to close our chapels; we defended them. So we guarded them day and night. He was opposed to receiving communion standing, being convinced that God wants us to receive communion kneeling.

Another problem I had with my associates was finances. They could not understand what was going on because inflation was great that year. Construction materials were inflated 500%. Food and other necessities rose about 300%. They had been accustomed to the prices before independence. When they saw my financial reports, it did not take them a long time "to realize that I was stealing money." They could not understand the changes that were taking place in the Church or in the society around them.

When I told Father Provincial how Father Šeškevičius was telling the parishioners to ignore my leadership, he said that he would move Father Šeškevičius. But Father Boruta did not do what he said he would do. With Father Boruta's many Church and civil responsibilities in Vilnius, I wondered how much time he had for the Jesuit community. There are many more details of the Klaipėda situation. One time Father Šeškevičius received a shipment of aid from Germany that included medicines. Father gave medicine to people without guidance from a doctor and, as a result, some people were poisoned. When Father Provincial was informed about this serious situation, he seemed to pay no attention.

I told Father Šeškevičius that he could not give out the medication in Church or on Church grounds, so he took it out into the street and gave it to the people giving them his instructions on dosage because he could read a little German. I was told that one of the women who had accepted the medicine from Father Šeškevičius took the medicine to her doctor before taking it and he told her that it was in suppository form. A friend of hers had already taken the medication orally. Many people became sick in the parish from the medication.

During his time in exile in Siberia, Father Šeškevičius would provide the Sacrament of Matrimony quickly as he visited the many villages in which Catholics lived. A priest may only come to the village every ten years and there were often many marriages to perform. He got in the habit of marrying people quickly as he visited their homes. When he was in Klaipėda working as parish associate, he continued to perform "Siberian marriages," even though we had a marriage preparation program established in the parish. On one occasion when he was visiting people who lived in the parish, he asked a woman if she wanted to accept the Sacrament of Matrimony. She responded that she did. He told her to stand next to the man who was in the apartment. "But, Father, he is my son. My husband is fishing in the Baltic Sea." As one ages it becomes increasingly difficult to judge the differences in age of those who are much younger than oneself. It was the biggest joke in the parish at that time. My letter to the Father General did not include any of the above-mentioned problems. Even in closing I wrote of only the hardship of having so many superiors:

While in Klaipėda, I had five superiors simultaneously. Bishop Antanas Vaičius was my superior for parish matters. Father Jonas Boruta in Vilnius was my Provincial. Father Leonardas Jagminas in Kaunas was my Novice master and I was to see him once a month in Kaunas. Father Antanas Šeškevičius, my assistant in the parish in Klaipėda, was assigned by Father Boruta as my spiritual director. I was also told that I was to go to confession to Father Šeškevičius. And Father Stasys Kazėnas in Šiauliai was my immediate or local superior. From the parish in Klaipėda, where I was assigned, all but one of these superiors were many kilometers away. With five superiors, each living in a different city, there were complications when among them they did not know what the other has said and done...
Sincerely in Christ, Rimantas Gudelis

After one month I received a reply from Father General telling me that he had received my letter and was studying the situation. After eight more months, I wrote another letter to Father General asking that my files be examined and that I needed an answer. But Father General is still studying the matter until today.

At that time Father Šeškevičius was very famous because he had spent 25 years in the Gulag. Provincial Boruta was one of the editors of *The Chronicle*. I was just a simple Jesuit novice. Currently the situation is different. Because of poor management, Boruta and Šeškevičius do not enjoy a positive image. They are not heroes of the new Church in Lithuania.

In 1993, I moved to the diocese where I was born and was given a new assignment to restore a camp that had been a young Communist summer camp. There were three tasks: first, to raise money; second, to restore the damaged camp and church dynamited by the Soviets; and third and most important, to develop Catholic summer youth programs and to find people to run them. During that time I had to deal with many institutions: the diocese, the Lithuanian Catholic Youth Federation *Ateitis*, who officially owned this camp, the city council, the Ministry of Education, and various foundations.

If I failed leading the biggest parish in Klaipėda, Lithuania, here I think that I succeeded in creating a camp atmosphere and building a modest church. We developed successful camp programs and were successful in raising money. This allowed me to renew the campsite. I found that when I gained formal and informal authority it was very easy to deal with government people, people from the educational system and people from the other non-Church oriented organizations. But, the biggest difficulty was dealing with those in the Church who were in the resistance against the Soviets. The Board of The Lithuanian Catholic Youth Federation *Ateitis* consisted of a president, five vice-presidents, and a spiritual director. There, I was one of the vice-presidents; most of the board came from those Church circles that had been committed to the resistance to the Soviet regime. Some of them had been imprisoned by the Soviets. This organization was successful between the two world wars and after independence was re-established. The former dissidents had much influence in society and took leadership roles in this organization, which created some problems. First, there was a lack of trust due to the way of thinking of most victims of the oppressive regimes. Furthermore, they were religious people from various conservative religious circles and that also created many difficulties.

In conclusion, one famous dissident described the times of persecution in these words: "During the occupation we resisted and survived very well. If we had a scale of one to ten, of course, we could not give this period a score of 'ten,' but we could give it at least a 'five.' We had those who resisted in the forests and in the Church, and we had those who sat in the KGB offices and persecuted people. But we had an intelligentsia as well: professors and teachers, and they showed a lot of wisdom, teaching under communist rule. We had many people in the economic sphere that skillfully built our country during that time. We have to remember them."

Times of transition brought more difficulties and misunderstandings in society as a whole, especially for those who were involved in the resistance movement.

CHAPTER TWO: OBSERVATION

A. Introduction

After *Perestroika*, when Lithuania became an independent country, a time of transition began. There was a need to reorganize life in a different way, which required much creativity, flexibility, experience and knowledge. Things did not always run smoothly; economic difficulties, government corruption, bank crisis, unemployment, crime, etc.

In 1997, I was assigned as an assistant pastor at a Lithuanian parish in Chicago. There is a large community of Lithuanian displaced persons in Chicago. During the time of Soviet occupation, they supported the dissident movement in Lithuania in various ways. The displaced persons in the U.S. printed *The Chronicle* not only in the Lithuanian language, but also translated it into English, Spanish, German, etc. They found ways to financially support *The Chronicle* editor in Lithuania during the Soviet Regime. These two sub-cultures, the dissidents in Lithuania and the displaced persons in exile, had much in common: the dream of an independent Lithuania and the minority status of dissidents in Lithuania and displaced persons in the United States. The Roman Catholic Church was significant for both groups, not only as an instrument of salvation, but also as a means for the preservation of national cultural identity.

During *Perestroika*, when such things became possible, many noted dissidents from Lithuania visited Lithuanian communities in exile, i.e., in the United States, Canada, and Australia. At that time they were regarded as National Heroes. In 1998, during a commemoration of Lithuanian Independence Day, one honored speaker of the Lithuanian displaced persons community, who supported the dissident movement very much, mentioned in his speech the many hardships Lithuania was going through. At the end of his speech he shouted, "Where are our dissidents now? They did a tremendous job resisting the Soviet regime. They may be able to help Independent Lithuania overcome the difficulties the country is experiencing now. Where are they?"

I was close to the dissident movement. The question this speaker raised provoked me to think about what was going on with the former dissident movement.

What role are they playing in independent Lithuania? How are they accepting the new changes in the country? Are they reconciled with their past? How are they looking to the future?

While I was thinking about what to research for my Doctor of Ministry project, another event happened. On the tenth anniversary celebration of our independence, February 16, 2000, President Valdas Adamkus, a former Chicagoan, gave a national award to a former KGB general and head of the KGB in Lithuania, Misiukonis. During the time that he was the head of the KGB, he participated in the killing of Lithuanian partisans, the oppression of Catholics, and ordering the use of chemicals to destroy people's health. But when the country was fighting for independence in the early '90's, he supported the independence movement. Being the interior minister then, which included being head of the police, he ordered the police to support an independent Lithuanian government. After the Soviet coup in August of 1991, he was removed from the government and became a very successful businessman. During the ceremony in the president's palace at which he was to receive the award, a dissident nun, Sr. Nijolė Sadūnaitė stepped up to the podium and started to shout, "Mr. President, you are awarding a killer!" This incident revealed clearly that our society is not reconciled. Wrongdoers are rewarded; victims are victimized a second time, and the naïve outsider (the President lived in the United States for 50 years) thinks that in this way it is possible to achieve reconciliation. This event reveals that our society is not reconciled and that it will be a long process, which needs to be discussed and studied.

B. Goal of the Interviews

The core of my study is a series of interviews with former dissidents who resisted against the Soviet regime. When speaking about dissidents, I have in mind the Lithuanian dissident movement within the Catholic Church, which began in the '70's. There were no dissident movements before this time because during Stalin's last years the most active people were killed or deported to Siberia. Later, Khrushchev gave a little freedom to the Church. Everyone was waiting to see how things would go. In 1961, Khrushchev passed a law that persecuted the Orthodox and Baptist Churches. After a few years, the oppression fell on the Catholic Church. The dissidents I am speaking about started their activities during this period. They organized their activities around three different groups: the Committee to Defend Catholic Rights in Lithuania, *The Chronicle of the Lithuanian Catholic Church*, which was the longest-published underground newspaper in the Soviet Union, and the Brothers of the Holy Eucharist, an underground organization to which I belonged.

When I started interviewing I had two purposes in mind - to listen and understand their experiences and by means of guided questions to help them to begin thinking differently about forgiveness and reconciliation. The goal of my interviews was to help the Lithuanian dissident group understand the theology and spirituality of reconciliation and to help develop a strategy within the Lithuanian Catholic Church towards forgiveness and reconciliation. The most helpful tool in the development of this strategy is the theology of reconciliation, which is, for the most part, unknown in this culture. Another tool is the experience of different cultures and churches and how they have dealt with the process of reconciliation. I chose this approach because I was part of the Church in resistance, and also the process of reconciliation always starts with the victim. If within the Lithuanian Catholic Church and society reconciliation is possible, I believed that the group who were dissidents (victims) could begin and lead the Church and society to reconciliation.

My pastoral experience and the first round of interviews showed me how difficult are the times of transition, how difficult it is to move from resistance to reconstruction of society. From the interviews with former dissidents, I learned that many of them are still living the spirit of resistance. For many of them the theology of reconciliation and spirit of forgiveness towards the former wrongdoers or for those who think differently from them is foreign.

The main purpose of this study shifted a little after I did the first round of interviews. It is important to help the Lithuanian dissident group to understand the theology and spirituality of reconciliation. Many of them are stuck in the past; being victims of the Soviet regime they have no strength for adaptation to new situations where we have to reconstruct society's moral order, yet not resist social change. After the first round of interviews I felt that the main task was to help develop a strategy and spirituality within the Lithuanian Catholic Church as whole towards forgiveness and reconciliation.

When I started to do my fieldwork, I thought the best thing for me to do was structured interviews. When I completed the first few interviews and asked them several prepared questions, I found one thing. The agenda of those questions and the agenda of the former Soviet regime victims were totally different. The agenda of my questions was about the reconciliation and what the Church has to do to help reconstruct a society after Soviet oppression. Usually, I found that the dissidents had different agendas. Even when I asked questions about the future, they continued to talk about the past. I asked about reconciliation, but when they answered, they were talking about revenge.

Then I moved from structured interviews to semi-structured interviews. Semi-structured interviews were based on a clear plan that I kept constantly in mind, but also characterized by a minimum of control over the informant's response. The idea was to get people to open up and to let them express themselves in their own terms, and at their own pace. I always had in mind to find where they stood in terms of reconciliation but allowed the conversation to be flexible. Finishing my interviews, I noticed one thing. One needs to be less structured if the interviewee is not reconciled or if the person has only begun to move towards reconciliation.[1]

I thought that the interviews would be the major source of information, but articles in the Lithuanian and foreign press about the dissidents and their own articles also tell a great deal and reveal where they are in the process. Because the people I interviewed were significant in society, there are many articles in the press about them and by them. At times differences are revealed between the interviews and the articles.

I will cite an example. During the interview session when the question was raised about reconciliation, the person says, "I am fine, I am reconciled." But in his articles he writes how we must punish communists and how during the Soviet regime it was easier because we always knew our enemy was. Right now we know that there are many problems, but we don't know who our enemy is.

Here is another example from the press, which will help to understand more easily where a former dissident is in the process of reconciliation. One former dissident spent many years in prison. After he came from prison, he was always assigned to the smallest parishes. After *Perestroika*, he immediately began to preach about reconciliation and forgiveness. He became a close friend of former Communist party leaders, when the rest of the dissidents, with few exceptions, supported only right wing political forces. They often paid him visits. He was invited to their meetings. He did these things to promote social reconciliation.

In 1992, his sermon was printed in the newspaper. The title of the sermon was: "If a Muslim were to Stop by Our Church these Days." Mentioned at the beginning of the sermon is the Gospel parable of the prodigal son and his father's love for him. Later on, the sermon speaks of a Muslim who, upon hearing this parable (read in all the churches in Lithuania during Lent) would have been amazed:

> And so, a Muslim hearing this lovely tale in our church and then reading our newspapers, which constantly write about "desovietization," [desovietization – a term used during the first years after independence demanding that those who had collaborated with the Soviet Government be removed from all responsible positions, be punished, and do penance. Before elections this term was always mentioned by the political parties on the right] would certainly marvel at it. Haven't thousands upon thousands

---

[1] See Bernard Russell, *Research Methods in Anthropology* (Thousand Oaks, CA: Sage Publications, 1995), 213-15.

of our sons, who had distanced themselves from our homeland, from the Church, now returned? Several years have passed since the majority has returned, and yet now we are chasing them away.

A Muslim could never fathom this. He would say: "Aha! The priests who told this parable, along with the bishops, should get into their cars (which many of them own) and drive over to picket at the Parliament to get them to stop this "desovietization" and, according to the teachings of the Gospel, welcome the sons who have returned, believe in them! After all, the parable clearly states: The fa-ther be-lieved!"

That's what a Muslim would have thought. And what would he think upon learning that even God-fearing Christians are instigating this horror of "desovietization," this horror of hatred and revenge? Perhaps a great many members of Parliament attend church. If so, then they have heard this parable, and yet they behave in the opposite manner of what is written in the Gospel, as if the words of the Gospel went in one ear and out the other. A Muslim would ask: "Then why do you read the Gospel if you do not heed it?" He would shrug his shoulders on his way out and say: "We DO adhere to the Koran!"

This sermon did not go unnoticed, even, as one might guess, at the highest levels of the Church hierarchy. In August 1992, the bishops of Lithuania issued a pastoral letter, which was to coordinate with the upcoming October parliamentary elections. The following is a portion of the bishops' letter in which the words spoken by this dissident at Easter resound like an echo:

In reference to the Gospel parable of the prodigal son, merely returning to the father's house and taking a seat at the table for the feast is not sufficient. The true celebration takes place in the house when he who has returned repents for his sins before his family. Common sense and political acumen should encourage former activists of the soviet system to boldly and publicly condemn all of their crimes and make right the offences committed against their victims. We are certain that they still have the opportunity for sincere penance and a change of lifestyle.[2]

Parish priests in Lithuania were asked to read this letter from the pulpit or

---

[2] Lietuvos kardinolas, arkivyskupas ir vyskupai (Lithuanian Bishops Conference), "Kuriant brolišką ir laisvą Lietuvą: Lietuvos vyskupų ganytojinis laiškas (Establishing a Brotherly and Free Lithuania: Lithuanian Bishops' Pastoral Letter),"*Lietuvos aidas*, No. 176 (6134), (09 September 1992): 1 and 5.

share its message. This was to be done on an assigned date: the second Sunday in September, just a few weeks before the election.

One may make a variety of comments upon the parable of the prodigal son. However, the tone of the pastoral letter, which calls for not only spiritual penance but political penance as well, speaks for itself. The Parable of the Prodigal Son is one of the most beautiful passages of Holy Scripture speaking of reconciliation. Lithuanian bishops at that time saw in this parable only the need to do penance. So it also is an indication that the theology of reconciliation in not known in the Church in Lithuania.

A year later, there was public reaction from the clergy and particularly from the former dissidents, and they wrote a petition stating that it is a very bad thing to talk and to collaborate with former communist leaders because they are still our enemy. This petition in 1993 was printed in many Lithuanian dailies with the signatures of 153 priests (21% of all clergy in Lithuania at that time), especially those who had resisted the Soviet regime. This helps to see where people are in the process of reconciliation. This position clearly shows that those who signed are not reconciled and that they are stuck in the past: because during the last decade of the Soviet regime, there was a petition "war." Every petition to Soviet officials demanding religious freedom was significant because it was printed in the western press and broadcast by radio stations such as Voice of America and Radio Free Europe. During the Cold War, the Soviet authorities tried to persuade Western nations that the Soviet Union is a free country. During this period, the petition "war" played a significant role. However, petitions were no longer effective after independence, when a complete restructuring of the social order was needed, not a petition "war." The 1993 petition showed that those former dissidents were stuck in the past and had no room to maneuver in a new situation. They resorted to old methods. It also shows that the dissidents who are now reconciled in our society became "dissidents" within the former dissident group.

Another factor that helped with my research was my social situation. I knew all of the people I interviewed years before. But, of course, there were differences between the dissident group and me. They had spent years in prison. They never had an education abroad except the education of the Soviet prisons. But, I think that in those interviews there was trust built between the dissidents and me, although many of them felt that I was different. They expressed this difference with this sentence: "Don't be spoiled by those western ideas and by those western Catholic universities." Because this sentence was repeated by dissidents whom I believe are not reconciled, it confirms my belief that they are stuck in the past and that for them new ideas are difficult to accept.

C. Ethics and Participant Observation

The goal of fieldwork should be the production of knowledge. The only value that is central in fieldwork is truth, but there are ethical issues surrounding every research, just as there are with any other form of human activity. Here, we consider ethical questions faced doing the interviews and fieldwork. I would like to discuss five issues: informed consent, privacy, harm, exploitation, and the possibilities for future research.

Informed consent

It is often argued that the people to be studied by social researchers should be informed about the research in a comprehensive and accurate way, and should give their unconstrained consent. The most striking deviation from this principle in the context of fieldwork is covert participant observation, where an ethnographer carries out research without most or all of the participants being aware that research is taking place. Some commentators argue that such research is never, or hardly ever, justified, that it is analogous to infiltration by agent provocateurs or spies.

Some settings would not be accessible to research, or at least not without a great deal of reactivity, if covert methods were not employed. All research falls on a continuum between the completely covert and completely open.[3]

In my interviews I struggled over whether I should be completely overt or covert. Because of the sensitivity of the issue of reconciliation, it is difficult to be completely open. If I would come to a person and ask directly about his reconciliation with his past, the answer would be always the same. "Yes, I am fine. I am reconciled." Speaking about informed consent, I had a struggle as to how open I could be in order to get as objective an answer as possible.

Privacy

In fieldwork there is information that is for public consumption and that which is secret or confidential. A frequent concern about research is that it involves making public things that were said for private consumption. And it is sometimes feared that this may have long-term consequences. The concept of privacy is complex. What is public and what is private is rarely clear-cut.

All my interviews were tape-recorded. There are a few very clear places where a person after he said a few sentences added that what he was saying was not for public use. But sometimes it was complicated to know what was private and what was

---

[3] Martyn Hammersley and Paul Atkinson, *Ethnography, Principles and Practice* (London: Oxford Press, 1995), 262-265.

public when the person being interviewed lowered his voice. For example, in one case, a person told in a quiet voice about a friend who was also a dissident, "I cannot understand why in prison he always worked in the bath, handing out underwear and we had to spend all our time down in the mines." Of course, with his low voice, he is indicating that this man in one way or another had collaborated with prison officials, because that was the only way to get the better jobs in the prisons. But because it was said in a low voice and with the indication that it was private, I did not think that I could use this for my study. But in some cases it was difficult to know if the interviewee meant the information to be private or public.

Harm

Harm may arise as a result of the actual process of doing research and/or through publication of the findings. At the very least, being a research subject can sometimes create anxiety or worsen it, and where people are already in stressful situations, research may be judged to be unethical on these grounds alone. Publication can damage the reputation of individuals, organizations, as well as hurting the feelings of those involved.

Without using names, we need to confront the situation, which presently exists in the Lithuanian Catholic Church. I think the approach taken where names are not given, but the theological method of "resistance towards renewal" is confronted, is justified. This study confronts the situation for the good of the Church and society.[4]

Exploitation

Normally researchers investigate those who are less powerful than they, and for this reason are able to establish a research gain to their advantage and to the disadvantage of those they study. The concept implies a comparison between what is given and received, and/or between what is contributed to the research, by each side. And yet, of course, most of the benefits and costs, and the relative contributions, cannot be measured, certainly on any absolute scale. Whether or not exploitation is taking place is always a matter of judgment, and one that is open to substantial possible disagreement.

There are problems surrounding judgments about what exactly constitutes exploitation. Participants should be empowered by becoming part of the research process; or that research should be directed towards studying the powerful and not the powerless. Such proposed remedies do not always avoid the problem, however; and

---

[4] Anthony Gittins, *Observant Participation: Ethics, "Hard Words," and Liturgical Inculturation* (Collegeville, Minnesota: The Liturgical Press, 1996), 139-41.

they are controversial in themselves.[5]

I do not think that in my case I can speak about the exploitation issue because the people I interviewed were my teachers 10 to 15 years ago and my role models. At present, I do not agree with those who are not seeking reconciliation in society and within the Catholic Church. It is a strange feeling to interview your former teacher because the person conducting the interview always has the advantage.

When one is writing about reconciliation or, in other words, how two Church groups are not reconciled, ethical questions are very important because of the sensitivity of the matter and the vulnerability of the people about whom we are writing. The main guideline can be these words from the New Testament: "We are allowed to do anything,' so they say. 'We are allowed to do anything' – but not everything is helpful. No one should be looking to his own interests, but to the interest of others." (1 Cor. 10:23-24) The main interest is the future of the Church and of society. There is no future for society without reconciliation.

D. Autobiographies

I interviewed dissidents who were very active in the resistance movement and in the Church during Soviet occupation. These activities gained them an authoritative position among the Lithuanian people during the Soviet regime. All of them spent long years in the Soviet Gulags or were persecuted by the Soviet authorities, who would not allow them to study, or to have jobs they wanted. They were likewise not allowed to travel and to live where they wanted. The names of such dissidents are well known in Lithuanian society even today. I do not want to disclose the names of the ten dissidents interviewed for this study because of the sensitivity of the matter and the vulnerability of the people about whom I am writing.

Here are some biographical features common to them. Many of them grew up on farms or in small villages and just a few in cities. Their parents and grandparents were mostly farmers or laborers, but a few came from well-educated families. In one way or another their families experienced Soviet persecution during the Stalin regime. Punishments included imprisonment, exile to Siberia, forced moves from town to town, the loss of or restrictions on their employment because of their political and religious beliefs. Some of them were imprisoned during Stalin's times, and again later during the last decades of the Soviet Empire. All of them were active as dissidents after 1970.

---

[5] Martyn Hammersley and Paul Atkinson, *Ethnography, Principles and Practice*, 269.

Joan Lofgren in her article *Reconciliation in the Shadow of the Soviet Past*[6] is talking about the process of reconciliation in Estonia. In her article she provides a paradigm: *Complicity as degree of commitment*, where she compares the commitment of the people in the Soviet Union to the Soviet regime:

| **Active collaboration** | **Passive collaboration** | **Acquies- cence** | **Passive resistance** | **Active resistance** | **Direct challenge** |

Former dissidents I have interviewed belong to active/resistance and direct/challenge groups. All of them grew up in families where religion was an important part of life. All of them believed that the Church should play the most important role in the fight for the nation's liberation from the Soviets. Consequently, because of these convictions they became very active in the Church:

> I was probably one of many from that generation of Lithuanians who came to religion through political opposition, the prism of cultural opposition to communism. One way or another, Lithuania was an occupied country. One way or another, Lithuania was a country separated from her natural partners in the Western world. On the other hand, I sometimes think that if I had lived in such an atheist society but that society hadn't been enslaved politically and nationally, it is entirely possible that the interest in religion, the influence of religion may not have been as strong as it was in Lithuania in those days.

Since they lived in the Soviet Union they themselves encountered and lived through all the moral and social evils that communism brought to Lithuania. The following quotation from the interview revealed two of them—the existence of a dual conscience and the lack of trust:

> Going to school became a pragmatic matter for me as well. For example, I become friends with the son of the chief officer of the KGB of the town. I can't remember his name. He was very bright and never got into

---

[6] Joan Lofgren, "Reconciliation in the Shadow of the Soviet Past" in Lucia Ann McSpadden (ed), *Reaching Reconciliation* (Uppsala, Sweden: Life & Peace Institute, 2000), 174.

fights. Later, he worked in Vilnius. But, for instance, whenever I would go to his house for dinner his father would ask me why I didn't bless myself before eating. I would reply that I didn't know how. Somehow from an early age it was clear to whom you could tell certain things and to whom you couldn't, as in this instance. Of course I couldn't tell how I came across, whether or not I was a convincing liar. Maybe this man saw right through me. But I absolutely knew that it was a necessity.

Here is another case:

The situation was quite interesting. Because it was a small town, the members of the intelligentsia: physicians, teachers, the pharmacist knew one another well. For example, my elementary school teacher's brother was a sacristan, and when the pressure for children to join the Pioneers started in town, they left "their own," the children of the intelligentsia, alone. But they absolutely terrorized the ordinary villagers in all sorts of ways. Of course, even that teacher used to go to church in secret. We would see her sitting in the small balcony just off the sacristy, but when it came time to sign up for the Pioneers, she would dictate the Pioneers' oath to us and then collect our papers. I myself wouldn't write anything down. And so, one of my conflicts of this type was that when she would begin the dictation I would try to get the other children not to write anything down either. She said that while I didn't have to write anything down, I was not to keep others from doing so. Of course, she handled the situation as best she could under the circumstances. That was second or third grade in elementary school. That's when that kind of pressure was on.

The lack of trust

How did you decide which priests not to trust?

Usually there were peculiar rumors. For instance, if you told something to a priest and those same words came back to you, even outside the scope of the KGB, then you would conclude that that priest was unreliable. Maybe he hadn't even been at fault after all, but to misjudge was very dangerous.

Are there some differences between priests you did not trust?

One would probably have to differentiate. There were those whom you couldn't trust. There were others whom you could trust cautiously. There are certain topics you'd be better off not discussing. Finally, there were those whom you could trust. So I would say there are three types of priests. Sometimes the suspicions were exaggerated. However, it was better to be safe than sorry. Also, there was one more thing we strive for: to know as little as possible about others. Even now it is difficult to trust priests.

E. Interviews with Former Dissidents

In the second part of this chapter we will discuss how the dissidents understand the meaning of reconciliation and where they are in the process of reconciliation after the atrocities committed against them. I will use the information I have from the interviews. As a result of the interviews, I found four different views:
    a. Reconciled without requiring justice (just one)
    b. Reconciled but requiring social justice
    c. As the disciples of Emmaus, still on the way to reconciliation
    d. Stuck in the past and has no reason or strength to move towards
    reconciliation.
Most of our dissidents belong to groups 'c' and 'd.' I chose to interview those who are reconciled because they became dissidents among the dissident group. I found that those groups have totally different views concerning many issues. Let us examine how the dissidents look at the following issues:

    a. Are they reconciled with the past?
    b. Wrongdoer and Forgiveness
    c. Is reconciliation possible in Lithuania?
    d. What kind of role can the Church play in the reconciliation process?
    c. Is the Bible talking about reconciliation?

a. Are you reconciled with your past?

During semi-structured interviews, much time was spent speaking about the past. Therefore it is probably for the following reasons that many of the interviewees are still "stuck in the past" and lack the capacity to maneuver in a new situation. Social changes in society and changes in the Church after Vatican II are very difficult for them to adapt to. There are many things they cannot understand or accept. In that way they are more comfortable talking about their past than they are about the future. Also, during the times of Soviet oppression, by belonging to the dissident movement, it gave them political and social stature in society. Especially with those who are not reconciled with the past, during interviews much time was spent talking about events that happened in the past. Those who were reconciled were more flexible talking about the present and the future of society and the Church. Let us start with the person who is on the way towards reconciliation. He gives a very exact description of what happened in the country, from the perspective of the reconciled person.

Many dissidents were clinging to the past and they had no strength to maneuver. They are like the disciples from Emmaus. They got lost and were afraid and did not recognize Jesus. Who helped you to free yourself from your past and find a new vision?

I feel uncomfortable when many dissidents are stressing how many good things they did. *Sodra* (pension fund) pays people who were in exile, for political prisoners, an additional pension. I have 139 litas (~ $35), which is just my pension. The addition to my pension I am not taking because I think that it was an honor for me to participate in the resistance. Many had families and they were not brave enough. Priests had to show courage and go to the Gulags. It is not honest to be proud about that right now.

But when the country became free, we must understand our situation. There were three sorts of prison: first, displaced persons' prison, I mean those who ran away from Lithuania and who lived in refugee camps in Germany; second, those who spent time in Vorkutos and Intos camps, most labor camps; third, the forgotten prison and most dangerous prison was *poviestka*, in Russian an invitation to come to the KGB office. Everyone had to go through that. All of us must say that we were prisoners.

Right now "patriots," or those who consider themselves patriots, I don't know why, cannot forgive. Without any rehearsal the people went to the Baltic Road, an action before independence, which protested occupation when people from Tallinn to Vilnius made a human chain. Let us think about our teachers, how they felt. I think that they were ashamed because they stayed at the church door and put down the names of children who attended church. I think that those teachers are ashamed right now. I think that from this third prison all prisoners should be liberated. Of course, I am not speaking of those who were killing others. Usually when there is a war, there are deserters who when captured are executed. When freedom comes, every State changes its attitude towards deserters. They are forgiving them. We had to do the same after our independence.

Another reconciled dissident gives the following explanation about his way towards reconciliation.

Our society always is looking for significant spiritual leaders, especially the resisters who resisted the Soviet regime. Right now it has been noted that some of them are not reconciled with themselves and it seems that they do not have any force for maneuvering in a new situation. You are the winner of the national prize for reconciliation. How did you achieve this award?

Answering this, I want to first of all explain to you how we are looking for solutions in conflict situations. It would be good that we believers, especially priests, saw those questions in the light of the gospels. We know that the first martyrs Sts. Stephen and Sebastian experienced a lot of wrongdoing but somehow they managed to escape from anger and revenge.

When I was in prison after WWII, I saw many good examples. Professor Karsavin was sentenced for nothing; he did not commit any crime. But he never created any plans for revenge. He created wonderful sonnets on religious topics. I was impressed with the rector of the Jesuit University, who later became a bishop. When he came back from exile during the German occupation, everybody thought that he would invite the Poles to have revenge on the Lithuanians. But from the pulpit of St. John's Church he said the following: "From old times we know that the biggest pleasure for the gods is revenge. But the names of the gods are not capitalized. Our God is the God of love. I am thankful that I experienced many atrocities. This helps me to understand what it means to love in a Christian way."

From the second group of people I received a totally different answer. Reconciliation was a difficult issue to deal with. They still lived in a spirit of revenge, requiring justice and punishment.

Those who deserted during the war were killed. After the war the state forgives the deserters. Maybe in our situation, social reconciliation, it would be better to forgive?

All that is possible. But those new Bolsheviks are people with evil will. They did not want good for Lithuania. They wanted to use the country and to steal. They don't need justice. They wanted to impoverish Lithuania and to destroy the economy so that we would ask again Russia for protection. They have no shame. They are propagating their baser instincts.

When I look at our society right now, I notice that it is as divided as it was ten years ago. The division is between those who collaborated and those who resisted. What do you think? Is it possible to start the process of reconciliation in Lithuania?

I think that you are using the wrong terms. We are not divided as a people, but the Soviets divided us. In 1990, the KGB general Eismantas said, "I will divide all of them." I did not believe him; but as I see right now, our society really is divided. All parties and organizations have infiltrated people. To reconcile, they need to return justice. Until justice is returned, our efforts are empty. If you want to reconcile people, you must reconcile them around somebody. It was told to us by the Soviets when we were in prison. Then we asked them around what they wanted us to reconcile. Around Jesus or around Marx? When we were told about Marx, we said that it was not good for us. When they said about Jesus, we said it was okay. The term "reconciliation" is not fit in our context as well as the term "dissidents" because we were fighters for freedom. Those who were afraid were silent or collaborated with the Soviet regime

During the interviews dissidents who are just on the road to reconciliation or stuck in their past always stressed justice. In a way they are right. Failure to pursue it is an illustration of this, meaning that the bureaucracies of the country continue to be dominated by communist functionaries who may throw sand in the gears of the fledgling democracy whenever possible. Former Communist activists, having had the economic potential of Lithuania in their own hands, privatized it through legal or illegal means and are again the masters of the situation. The majority of the dissidents said: "Justice is needed first before true reconciliation can occur." But what does the Gospel say?

Walter Wink, in his book *Reconciliation in the Healing of Nations*, talks about justice and reconciliation. He says that, "this is a sentiment with which people in many transitional nations would concur. Yet at the same time, Christians are commanded to love their enemies, not after justice has been secured (it rarely is, at least fully), but right in the midst of the struggle. Is it necessary to distinguish between societal

63

reconciliation, which waits on justice, and personal forgiveness, which individuals are capable of achieving? Or is that simply a dodge to avoid taking love seriously? Are only certain saints capable of forgiveness and reconciliation, or is it a demand laid on all Christians? If Christians exempt themselves from the necessity of forgiveness, how can they ask it of anyone else? Unless reconciliation is built into the struggle from the outset, it becomes exceedingly difficult to appeal for it at the end. It is, of course, natural to hate and refuse to forgive. The gospel, however, is not natural."[7]

b. The Wrongdoer and Forgiveness

Who was a wrongdoer during the Soviet regime? Joan Lofgren, in her paradigm *Complicity as conformity*[8] (to state/ system), distinguishes three categories of collaboration in Soviet Estonia:

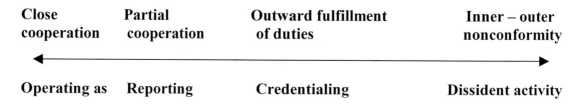

Close cooperation	Partial cooperation	Outward fulfillment of duties	Inner – outer nonconformity
Operating as	Reporting	Credentialing	Dissident activity

After forty-five years of Soviet occupation, many families in the country had at least one member involved in at least one of the three types of compromising activity. Does membership in the Communist Youth Organization – *Komsomol*, which was virtually mandatory for admission to a university, count as a crime, or simply an empty gesture? Many had to report to the KGB or Communist Party leaders for one reason or another. What should be done in this situation? To prosecute or fire a handful of scapegoats could in no way cleanse the past, and to prosecute or fire everyone who was guilty would render the state inoperable. In many cases people were forced to betray. Here is an example from interviews.

---

[7] Walter Wink, *When the Powers Fall* (Minneapolis: Fortress Press, 1998), 52.
[8] Joan Lofgren, "Reconciliation in the Shadow of the Soviet Past" in Lucia Ann McSpadden (ed), *Reaching Reconciliation* (Uppsala, Sweden: Life & Peace Institute, 2000), 174.

Are there any former KGB agents who apologized to you?

I know little about that because I was betrayed by Lithuanian partisans. Somebody betrayed them and they were arrested. During the investigation they were tortured and they told about my activities. Who betrayed me, partisans or those who tortured the partisans? How I was betrayed. I often heard the confessions of partisans. When they were arrested, some of them told that I did that when they were interrogated. So I was sent for ten years to prison. They betrayed me because of torture not because of bad will. Even now I know big intellectuals, poets, who during torture betrayed other people. Right now they are highly respected; they are heroes.

Yes, it is very difficult to distinguish in our situation who is a wrongdoer and who is a victim.

Of course, there are different people. We cannot paint in one color all the wrongdoers. They are very different. Sometimes even those who fought for Lithuanian independence committed crimes. Sometimes they committed crimes in order to have better jobs and better positions. A priest I know who betrayed many partisans is mentally ill. The KGB convinced him that every government is from God. If you serve us, you will serve God. He believed that.

It is not a big secret that many priests collaborated with the Soviet regime. They collaborated to gain a better position. On the other hand, now many dissidents are looking for revenge, not for reconciliation. We have a difficult situation in the Church right now. Is this situation in which nobody seeks reconciliation and when the wrongdoers are never punished, painfully affecting the Catholic Church? What do we have to do?

You see, collaboration has a very bad meaning. If the collaborator was one who betrayed people and for that reason they were killed, it is a crime. In that case, our justice system should sentence those people. But in one other way, everyone had to live under Soviet rule. For example, it was forbidden to teach the catechism to children. One group strongly resisted and fought this law. Another group looked for a solution, how to catechize the children quietly. I know a former agent who is now a very respected pastor. He put his signature on the collaboration document in exchange for permission to enter the seminary. He never collaborated in a real way. Can we call this collaboration a big crime or not? He was told that unless he collaborated he would not become a seminarian. It was during the Soviet regime that a kind of dialogue existed concerning how to deal with the oppressor, in a way of confrontation or quietly doing this for the good of the Church. Now when we are measuring everything we must be very careful.

One group of priests collaborated for honored positions in the Church or better financial positions. Another group did not agree to cooperate and they were placed in non-strategic small parishes. Even now there is tension between these two groups. What do we have to change?

It depends on how we look at the situation. Of course, we had those who for a piece of gold or a spoonful of better food collaborated. That is a very weak spot in our Church. It seems that it is very bad that we had those people. I know a few who were that type. But they did the job, fixed the churches; I do not think that they did great harm to the Church.

What I experienced personally was that if you did not become one of them as one KGB officer told me, you would go where there are white bears (i.e. Siberia) and you would die there. The KGB explained to me that it would be a big loss for the Church if I went there. They knew how to convince people. And we had those whom they convinced. What should we do with them? Condemn them? As Christians, we cannot condemn them. I really feel sorry for them but I cannot condemn them.

From the various viewpoints it is very difficult to ascertain whether the person who betrayed others was a victim or a wrongdoer. It is difficult to judge if a person who used to give information to the KGB did so out of conviction. Was it the best way to survive under the circumstances, involving the persecution of the Church and the Lithuanian people, or was it done seeking a career or profit?

One thing is very clear: that ten years after the reestablishment of independence wrongdoers are "disappearing" and more frequently one hears fine reports that the wrongdoers, as they were collaborating and giving information to the soviet leaders, were doing so out of concern for the future of the Lithuanian nation and Church. Wrongdoers in our society have such a tendency "to disappear." I believe that with few exceptions wrongdoers knew what they were doing.

Later excerpts from interviews reveal first of all how those dissidents who have been reconciled or who are on the road to reconciliation look at wrongdoers and at the issue of forgiveness.

When did you hate your perpetrator the most?

That never happened for me. Even that thought never came to me. I think that I was always in euphoria because for your sermons, for the Gospels, you can get such an award. For me it is not punishment. It is an award. I was not punished for corruption or robbery. And then in the gulag you always have something to do. You have no time to think. You must work and in that way make your bread. After events in Hungary I had another happy time in the Gulag in Vorkuta.

Do you know any situation where the oppressor took the first step towards reconciliation?

No, I don't know. Victims should take the first step. Take, for example, the relationship between the Polish and the German priests. Twenty percent of the Polish priests went up the chimneys of Auschwitz. After WWII the Communist government tried to make propaganda of that. But the Polish bishops wrote at that time, "We want to reconcile with the German nation..." With regard to those who hanged people, the same was done by the Russian Orthodox Patriarch in Berlin.

Did some of your oppressors or persecutors apologize for what they had done?

I just have a letter from the Supreme Court of independent Lithuania that both sentences were illegal and unjust. When they sentenced me for my activities, one hundred people gave false witness against my family and me. But nobody apologized to me, neither the prosecutors nor judges.

When did you hate most your oppressor?

I don't know. For me it seems that I did not have a sense of hatred. Of course, it was very uncomfortable when they persecuted me, when someone betrayed me, but I never experienced a hatred for them.

Did some of your persecutors apologize to you for what they had done to you?

From the perpetrators, I had none. I had a few cases when the KGB pressed people to talk about my activities. For example, one woman was forced to write a false article about me and she did it. She came to me later and said that she was really sorry. But those who did a systematic persecution do not even think about what they did.

Here is another interview with another group who find it difficult to forgive.

Tell me when during the Soviet regime you hated your oppressors. Maybe you can give their names.

Then I did not feel any hatred. But right now I am very angry at them.

Maybe you can explain why that happened.

Then everything was clear. There were two camps. One camp was atheists and those who occupied our country and they knew it was their job. The other camp was those who resisted against atheization and occupation. Everybody has his own position. Right now the same oppressors are carrying the Lithuanian flag and oppressing us more economically than in Soviet times.

Did anyone who persecuted you apologize?

Yes, one person did. It was my prosecutor. He called me and said, "Reverend, Do not hang up. Now I understand that when I persecuted you, I did the wrong thing." I told him, "I forgive you; and if you serve Lithuania well, I will help you. But with the condition to serve well." He promised. But, later when he became a member of Parliament, he never voted with the right wing people. He always voted with the communists. So he did not fulfill my condition so now I am free to talk. There were other cases. The KGB officer has a very high pension right now. He lives in Vilnius. At the end of my term in prison, he came to say a word of apology to me. As he gave me his bloody hand, he said that he had had no opportunity to act differently. Of course, he had no opportunity, he had to imprison people. And, of course, I had no opportunity. I had to sit in the prison. There was another one who was a prosecutor and who arrested me. Right now he has a very good job. He is the vice prosecutor in one of the biggest cities in Lithuania. I should probably tell this to journalists.

What, in your opinion, should we do about former collaborators ?

We should have courts and explain to all of them how many evil things they did. It is not important to imprison them. To imprison them is a very easy thing. But we would make martyrs of them. The courts should force them to do penance, not imprisonment.

We should have rebuilt to social justice but that never happened. The Bolsheviks took all our money. And right now they do what they like. We have underground casinos. We have underground bordellos. We have to fight and regain our rights. What have we done up to now? We have just begged for humanitarian aid. If we don't fight, nothing will happen. Morality has been destroyed. We need bishops who will lead during our lives and would have a strong voice.

On American television there was a program about Archbishop Tutu and his part in the process of reconciliation. In one of the meetings they questioned the former wife of Nelson Mandela because it was known that she participated in apartheid. At the beginning she did not say that she did that but when the Archbishop showed signs of reconciliation and forgiveness and started to cry, she then said that she was a wrongdoer. It is very difficult for the wrongdoer to admit that he did wrong. As you said, nobody apologized to you. But maybe you know somebody who did that in Lithuania?

No, I really don't know of any such instance and my friends don't, either.

What do you think? Can the wrongdoer take the first step toward reconciliation?

I imagine that they are Mafia, very terrible Mafia. It is the Mafia of Satan. They did not want to forgive me because their first enemy was God and religion. In Rome, during a conference I attended, former Soviet dissident Alexander Men was asked what he could say about Russian communists. Had they converted or just pretended to? He answered this question with another question, "Can the animal, who for 50 years walked on four legs, stand up and walk on two legs?"

Another discovery showed that those dissidents who are reconciled believe that the process of reconciliation should start with the victim. However those who are not reconciled think that the wrongdoers should take the first step towards reconciliation.

c. Is Reconciliation Possible in Lithuania?

Lithuania had to start reconstruction from scratch. It is different than in other Eastern European countries where they have government structures, diplomatic core, etc. Lithuania was under Soviet rule. A country with nothing had to create its own government, and other institutions having no experienced people. Those who did have experience had to collaborate with the Soviet regime in one way or another.

The larger part of the KGB archives was destroyed or taken to Russia. In all the eastern European countries, files regarding wrongdoing were left in the country. In Eastern Germany, tens of thousands have been fired from their jobs, 50,00 have been charged, and 180 convicted. By 1994, Bulgaria had removed from office some 9,000 top managers of enterprises, 14,000 officers in the state security agency, 90 percent of the government administration, and one third of all diplomats.[9] In Lithuania little was done. One journalist stated that the KGB files left in Lithuania contain enough material to determine whether this or that person collaborated, but not enough evidence that he was a wrongdoer. In many instances "the wrongdoer is gone." How can this situation be reconciled?

After 10 years of independence, the law of lustration was passed. The law of lustration states that everyone who collaborated with the KGB must register with a commission and admit that he/she was a collaborator. If he/she does not do this, everything that the commission finds will be made public. What do you think about this commission? Do you think that this commission will reconcile our divided society?

> I think that the main purpose is that those who collaborated will not have important places in the current government. The commission will decide after six months if those who came to them and confessed about their collaboration will be able to keep their jobs.

I can see some problems here. Within those years it was possible for much misinformation to be in the KGB archives. In these cases, people who were in competition for a job with the informant could have been falsely accused. What is your opinion? Is it too late to do this? And the job of this commission can lead society not

---

[9] Walter Wink, *When the Powers Fall*, 50.

towards reconciliation but toward division?

Yes, it is too late. It would have been better if we had done this ten years ago. But those things are still important today. Let them clean up their consciences, right now instead of never. It would be a clear cut with their past. Or if they will not do this, they will not repent. There will always be a possibility for them to think that they did the right things.

These days the process of liberation is going on in the world. After liberation in Latin America, Africa, finally the last colonial empire fell with the collapse of the Soviet Union. People in the former Soviet Union are divided into two groups: oppressed and oppressors. How do you think that the process of reconciliation should go? Who first should start the process of reconciliation, the oppressed or the oppressors? Or maybe this process is not possible at all?

It is hard to imagine how the process of reconciliation can occur. Those who were the oppressors have become the richest group of our society. Psychologically, it is hard to imagine that they would start the process of reconciliation. They are now trying to adapt to new conditions, to take the better positions in our society, and, to a certain extent, to oppress people once again, mostly economically.

Those who used to be oppressed, as I know them, have no anger. They are quick to forgive if the oppressors show signs that they have repented, signs that they are changing their lives. But anyway, the situation is very complicated and we need a lot of time.

Many nations had the same problem- in Latin America, in South Africa. Right now they are trying to reach reconciliation. What must we do in Lithuania?

Reconciliation without penance, without trying to improve oneself, is not reconciliation. That is just an insult to our feelings because those who were oppressed and will be oppressed and the oppressors will do in the future what they want to do. What kind of unity is here? As the Holy Father said where there is no justice there can be no peace. First of all, we must reconstruct justice.

And how can we come to reach a solution in Lithuania and in all Eastern Europe?

71

Only God can help us. For human beings it is too complicated because evil is very strong. Within those 70 years of the Soviet regime this evil is in all sectors of our society from the top to the bottom. They are controlling everything: the economy, the media, etc.

After those answers I still have a question: is reconciliation possible in post-communist Lithuania? Let us look at the reconciliation fund *Santarvė*. This fund was established to honor those who are seeking reconciliation within Lithuanian society. Those establishing this fund were mostly left-wing political individuals. The situation is very interesting in that former "wrongdoers" or those who profited from the situation in Soviet Lithuania showed a sign of reconciliation.

At the beginning they honored a few dissidents who were seeking reconciliation in our society; Cardinal Vincentas Sladkevičius, a few priests. Poets, scientists and politicians who worked in that area were honored as well. Because just a few are talking about reconciliation today in Lithuania, the fund has a problem of who to honor. I think last year they honored an individual who had no knowledge of reconciliation and had done nothing to encourage reconciliation in our country. They had even discussed honoring the Lithuania national basketball team!

Here are two opinions of how some reconciled dissidents who were honored and those who are reconciled but have not been honored see this fund:

This year you received the national award of reconciliation. A few years ago another dissident won this award. Could you tell what the reasons were that this award was given to you?

> Msgr. Vasiliauskas is a very bright man. In our capital he is doing a wonderful job. What can I say about myself? From the first day of independence I am going in the same direction. Some priests and friends even gave me the name "Communist." Some of them collected petitions saying that I was doing a bad job because I was talking with Communists and our former oppressors. Former Communist leader Brazauskas often came to my place. He said that only a minority of the people in the Communist party were wrong doers. And others needed to collaborate with the Communist regime to survive. I agreed with him. Their collaboration helped Lithuania. We don't have many Russian Communist people because Lithuanian Communists held positions that helped Lithuania. Russia did not send many ideological Communists. This is the reason that I don't hate the former Communists.

What I have to say about reconciliation is that the Church did not fulfill its mission of reconciliation. Maybe with one exception, that of our Cardinal who on the occasion that the Cathedral in Vilnius was returned to the Church said "Don't step on each other's heels. Don't throw stones at each other. We need stones to reconstruct our society, not for throwing them at each other. Let us grow little by little."

There is another group of dissidents, who suffered a lot. But they disagree with you; for them it is very difficult to reach reconciliation. What do you think about them?

Yes, they often are repeating the one word, "penitence." During meetings with people they are often asking me about that. It is difficult for me to answer in public. I am just saying that they probably forgot the second part of the "Our Father" prayer "and forgive those who trespass against us."

I have a hunch that some of our dissident priests are now becoming a burden to reconciliation.

I cannot respond for them. One thing that I require from priests is forgiveness.

In Lithuania we have a national prize of reconciliation. Over several years this prize was given to three priests, our Cardinal, Father Stanislovas, and Msgr. Vasiliauskas. But they are somewhat rejected by the larger group of our resistors. What are the dynamics that you see here?

One thing about this prize is that the committee who chooses the recipient is made up of people who in one way or another had relationships with the former Soviet regime. When former dissidents show signs of reconciliation as these three have done, they are more likely to receive this honor. If all dissidents go in this direction, the Church would have more influence and greater authority in our society these days. The other groups of dissidents still hold to the principles of the Old Testament, "eye for an eye" and "tooth for a tooth." They are demanding that those who committed those crimes should apologize. In other words, they are demanding that non-Christians behave as Christians. In that case they will be in opposition and be dissidents forever.

Opinions of those who are still on the way towards reconciliation or stuck in the past were different.

In Lithuania we have a national prize of reconciliation. Our cardinal and two priests have received this prize. What do you think about this prize? Maybe this prize is one of the signs used to consolidate our society?

> I think that this is not very serious. First of all, we must reconstruct justice and then talk about reconciliation. Or if someone is just talking about reconciliation without justice, then these are nice words, but they are lies. Let us pray that those who have established this prize were really concerned about reconciliation. I think that those priests were used for other purposes. But it is difficult here to talk about reconciliation.

Last year the prize of reconciliation was given to one of the dissidents. How can you interpret the fact that this prize was given to a former dissident who is seeking reconciliation right now?

> It is very hard to answer because he is a priest and a Capuchin. God gave us a different understanding. I don't know his life situation and what motivations he has. But I know that people are blackmailed now as they were in Soviet times

The history of this fund confirms that reconciliation should begin from the victim.

d. What kind of role can the Church play in the Reconciliation Process?

When we started to speak about the Church, both groups agreed that ten years after independence, the Church experienced some difficulties, but their opinions were totally different. Those who are not reconciled saw the problem not in the Church itself, but in society and in the people. During the Easter greeting one of them expressed this opinion:

> Ten years ago the wave of rebirth led many people to the Church and that created the illusion that the Church would no longer have to go to Golgotha, and that no one would dare to crucify her. However they were deceived. The Church, faithful to Jesus Christ, must always be prepared to

74

accept the role of her Founder, namely that she would always have to endure humiliations and be crucified, but also that she subsequently would surely arise renewed and filled with life.

There will always be people who support destructive sects, attempt to restore paganism, or deliberately ignore the most beautiful initiatives of the Church. To a true Christian it will always be amusing to hear the naïve announcements about the great and the small ratings of the Church, statistics about the increase and decrease of the numbers of believers, because the Christian understands that the Church is Christ, and if that is true, then the Church must suffer, die, and rise.

In these words you can find mistrust. There are many generalizations about other religious denominations; all of them are called sects. He is speaking more about suffering and fighting, in spite of the fact that it was on the day of resurrection. Many former dissidents think that the Church cannot help the process of reconciliation.

What kind of role can the Church play in the reconciliation process?

Reconciliation is very nice but it should begin with the wrongdoers; they should start. Those who were part of the occupational regime must be the ones to start. But what are they doing right now? They continue to lie, to steal, to misinform people, spreading hatred and hopelessness among the people. The process of reconciliation should start with them. It is a need that those people have for someone to forgive them, but they must show signs that they want to correct their own lives. But not one of them asks for forgiveness. Nobody recognizes that they were wrongdoers. It is opposite. They are happy that they worked for the KGB.

The other groups who are reconciled have a broader view of the Church and its future. Here is an interview with one of them:

If we look from the Christian position, we understand that in our country we need reconciliation. Who should start this process first, the oppressors or the persecuted?

If we go from the position of justice, the oppressors should be first. But from the Christian position, we can understand that our oppressors as non-Christians cannot step forward first. Unless somebody forces them and they are doing it out of fear. But because we did not have the law of lustration, no one did a gesture of repentance. I as a Christian think that we cannot demand that non-Christians came first to reconciliation. It would be the same as to demand that reptiles fly. I think that the process of reconciliation needs to be started from the Christian side. We must not seek revenge but must extend a hand of reconciliation to our oppressors and begin the process.

We are celebrating the tenth anniversary of our independence. Almost all dissidents were organized around the Catholic Church. What do you think about our dissidents right now? Are they helping in the process of reconciliation?

I think that some of them did and some of them did not take steps toward reconciliation. I think that those who took the steps were too slow and too weak. The situation is that we cannot demand that the other side begin the process of reconciliation. We have to show an example. We must take the first step because a non-Christian cannot do that.

During the Soviet regime many people supported the Catholic Church because the Church resisted the Soviet regime. After independence it seems that the Church is still looking for its own vision. What do you think is the essential thing for the Church to do today?

The Church was started by Jesus, and one of the main goals of the Church is to heal. Patients need a healer. Another thing is that the Church is a family. It is possible to say that in the Church there are parents, kids, brothers and sisters. If we go to the social sphere or the political sphere, we can talk as well about the healing function of the Church. What was the main disease in our society during the Soviet regime? The loss of spirituality- when spiritual values were placed in second or third place or absolutely denied, the Church helped fill this vacuum for many people. Because spirituality is closely connected to love of neighbor and human rights, the Church had a strategy to fight for human rights and for that gained great authority in society. The Church was supported as well as by those who did not practice the Catholic faith because they sympathized with what the Church was doing.

The time of oppression ended. With freedom we have new problems. Human rights are not the number one problem because it is guaranteed by our constitution and by international law, but we are facing other difficulties. People sometimes are unhappy because the disease still exists. I can tell that our society has depression. Society has freedom but does not know how to use it. There is no sense of solidarity or friendship. It shows that this disease that we had during Soviet times is not gone. It is simply that the situation changed, but the disease still exists, and nobody thinks about spiritual healing. We can tell that the spiritual healing of the Church is not going very well.

There are many possibilities. During independence we are free, and we must look for different ways to prevent this spiritual disease, how to stop this negative process. Today we have one side that is fighting for absolute freedom, freedom without any responsibility. From the other side there is the position of the Church and the faithful, which states that freedom exists only with responsibility. Confrontation between these two views has not lessened since independence.

When we look at the process inside the Church on the parish or diocesan level, we notice that there is one group who collaborated or were silent and profited and another group, which resisted. Inside the Church, reconciliation has not taken place between these groups. Often, wrongdoers still hold high positions in the Church and are having a negative influence. Another thing that I have noticed is that there are dissidents who did not reconcile with themselves and with today's situation. This creates tensions in the Church. This is my opinion. Can you agree with this opinion? What should the Church do in the future? What should the strategy be?

The Church, like the medical profession, has members who are honest and those who are not. During the Soviet regime, there were honest priests and not very honest priests. Saying it more concretely, they were demoralized. They just performed the priests' function. Other priests infiltrated as KGB agents. As spiritual healers, they could not perform their role. They did not attract people but the opposite. The same situation exists with those priests now.

If we look wider, there were Catholics who collaborated with the regime as well. Many Catholics allowed their children to join atheistic organizations. An absolute majority of the kids belonged to the atheistic organizations, Youth Pioneers, *Komsomol*, etc. Those people still exist, and they did not change much. The healing of the Church is a long and difficult process. How the Church accomplishes this depends on the hierarchy of the Church. In our days the situation has radically changed. During the Soviet regime we had to look to one thing, and today we need not those who fight but those who would reconcile. During the process of spiritual healing, we don't need fighters, we don't need volunteers to go to prison. We don't need those who are stubborn in their own positions, those who condemn others. In previous times there was a need because it was a way to resist and it was connected with one's political position. These days it is useless, and the Church has to find a way to heal itself differently.

And I see three new directions. The first is catechization. Sometimes it is very strange that ordinary believers are interested and can have a dialogue and can confront new sects and can confront their theology. And for the priests it is too complicated. They have a tendency to isolate themselves. I think that, in a certain sense, they need healing as well. We must have a dialogue, and it shows that catechization is one of the most important things. Catechization of the priests and the parishes is needed to know our faith better. If we don't know our faith, we cannot be faithful to God's great commandments. If a doctor is without qualifications, then he is just a dog doctor. Here, we have many of that kind of doctor.

Second, we have to create communities. The spirit of community is very weak. How to create a Christian community when political beliefs are put in first place? Now we need a different point of view. It is not important to what party he or she belongs. It is more important whether he/she is a good person or not. It is important if he/she wants to know God and share his experience or not. If we value the people through narrow political principle and propagate that, then the healer will become a healer of just one small group and not of all society. Priests cannot be part of any political groups, supporter of any political party, but must be a healer for all society. The Church has this disease, which must be treated.

Third, the Church must have a dialogue with everybody who needs spiritual help. All of them should be our clients. Those people must not be rejected by our action and angriness.

It is sad that this opinion is in the minority.

e. Does the Bible talk about Reconciliation?

What words in the Holy Bible or Jesus Christ's words encourage you to seek reconciliation?

If you forgive, then you will be forgiven. As I mentioned in the examples of Stephen and Sebastian, if I start to seek revenge, I will create a distance between God and myself, between the gospels and myself. For me it is very natural to not seek revenge.

What texts from the Bible would you use for confirming your theology towards reconciliation in our situation?

>Forgiveness will be won by those who forgive. The question of justice we must leave up to God. I understand forgiveness through the example of Christ. Christ accepted the injustice and evil around Him and was able in that environment to give love and reconciliation. Every Christian must act in that way.

In South Africa, Archbishop Tutu said that the wrongdoer is a weak man, that he cannot forgive. I, as a victim, must first show a sign of reconciliation. It is a very difficult process in South Africa. Is there any possibility that we can learn from the Archbishop's words in our Eastern European context?

>In Lithuania, as I know, we have already forgiven everyone. Even during the court process we are saying that we love and forgive them. We have nothing against them as human beings. I think that other dissidents did the same.
>
>But I think that this kind of forgiveness is useful. If you can see the opposite side, there are two-faced people. It is as Judas and Christ. Christ showed forgiveness, but Judas was left with his own ideas. When he betrayed, he did not repent. He did not say, "I am sorry" to Jesus. Our forgiveness is that we are not angry with them, but we want them to stop doing wrong. Forgiveness sounds too big for me. Even Jesus on the cross did not forgive those who did not ask for forgiveness. To forgive them for what they did to me—I can. But if those people did not show signs of improvement and they are making fun of, those whom they oppressed, calling our fighters for independence "bandits," and praising those who worked for the KGB, then it is difficult to forgive because forgiveness goes together with justice.

During the interviews the dissidents spent the most time talking about the past. The most difficult question was: Does the Bible talk about reconciliation? Even those who are reconciled somehow found it difficult to answer. Dissidents who are not reconciled, instead of finding texts about forgiveness, found that the Bible talks against forgiveness. One of them interpreted the text from Exodus as being against forgiveness. He said that they, like the Jewish people, must spend 40 years in the post-communist desert until a new generation comes.

After completing the interviews, I found that the idea of reconciliation is foreign to many of the dissidents. Knowledge of the Theology of Reconciliation is quite limited.

CHAPTER THREE:
THEOLOGICAL REFLECTIONS

Introduction

First of all, Lithuanian society and the Church, as well as science and theology, were cut off by the Iron Curtain from the Western World. During the time when Lithuania was isolated, many new dynamics happened in the world, as well as in the Church. One of these dynamics is the Theology of Reconciliation, a new development in theology, which started in recent decades. The need for a Theology of Reconciliation emerged because of changes in the world.

When the colonial system fell apart, when dictatorship and regimes collapsed in Latin America, Asia and in Africa, there was a need to develop a theology dealing with reconciliation after the oppression. The fall of the Soviet Empire left society divided as well: those who profited from the regime and those who suffered from it. In these situations the Church was to respond. Old-fashioned imperialistic theology did not fit here. There was a need for something new which promoted the development of the Theology of Reconciliation.

The Theology of Reconciliation is not known in Lithuania, even after one decade of independence and after the collapse of the Soviet Union. Even those people I interviewed knew from their own spirit that they needed to be reconciled with their past. For them it was difficult to find theological texts or Biblical images, which would give them a view of reconciliation.

One of the barriers was language. As many of those who are interested in theology could read only Lithuanian or Russian, they found it difficult to read new materials because this new material had not been translated into Lithuanian or Russian. In Church circles the word reconciliation is understood only in the narrow meaning of the word referring to the Sacrament of Reconciliation, confession.

Nobel prize winner Archbishop Desmond Mpilo Tutu, in his book *No Future Without Forgiveness*, writing about the importance of the Theology of Reconciliation notes: "Theology helped us in the Truth and Reconciliation Committees to recognize that we inhabit a moral universe, that good and evil are real and that they matter. They are not just things of indifference. This is a moral universe, which means that, despite all the evidence that seems to be to the contrary, there is no way that evil and injustice and oppression and lies can have the last word. For us who are Christians, the death and resurrection of Jesus Christ is proof positive that love is stronger than hate, that life is stronger than death, that light is stronger than darkness, that laughter and joy, and compassion and gentleness and truth, all these are so much stronger than their ghastly counterparts."[1]

The long isolation from the Christian world and the language barrier did not allow for the Lithuanian Church to understand how different churches contributed to reconciliation, as reconciliation took place in other parts of the world such as Africa, Latin America and even Eastern Europe. In the limited space available, we will explore the Theology of Reconciliation, which most closely corresponds to the situation in Lithuania. We will attempt to explore what biblical texts say about this topic using John Paul Lederach and the theologians Robert Schreiter, Margaret Mitchell, Miroslav Volf, Seyoon Kim, Walter Wink, Gregory Baum, and Harold Wells. We will also give some examples of how the Church in different parts of the world dealt with the process of reconciliation and explore how those examples can contribute to promoting deeper thinking about different strategies of reconciliation.

A. Jacob's Journey Towards Reconciliation

Let us begin with the Old Testament. During my interviews, just one interviewee spoke using the image of the Old Testament. Even when the question was asked about the Biblical texts dealing with reconciliation, he spoke of an opposite image saying that the story of Exodus tells us in our situation that we are like Jews fleeing from Egyptian exile. God did not allow the chosen people to enter the Promised Land for 40 years until the enslaved generation was dead. Maybe this interviewee was right. He is correct in one sense that the process of reconciliation is a long journey.

But the Old Testament has wonderful stories about reconciliation as well. It is Jacob and Esau's journey towards reconciliation, about which John Paul Lederach writes in his book *The Journey Towards Reconciliation*. Here is a narrative of this story (Genesis 25-33):

---

[1] Desmond Mpilo Tutu, *No Future Without Forgiveness* (New York: Doubleday, 1999), 86.

Esau and Jacob are brothers, sons of Isaac and Rebecca. Esau is the firstborn, the hunter, and the pride of his father's eyes. Jacob stays near home and close to his mother. When Isaac is old and nearly blind, he calls Esau to bless him as the firstborn son.

Esau sets out to hunt for game to roast for the meal preceding that generational blessing. While he is gone, Rebecca shows Jacob how to trick the old man into believing he is Esau. Not knowing and not seeing, Isaac bestows the revered blessing on his younger son, Jacob.

When Esau returns and brings the meal to his father, they both discover that they have been tricked. Esau moans with an "exceedingly great and bitter cry." He implores his father three times, "Bless me, me also, father. Have you not reserved a blessing for me? Have you only one blessing, father? Bless me, me also, father!" (from 27:34-38). But there is nothing further that Isaac can give. He has already released the blessing for the firstborn; like an arrow in flight, it cannot be recalled-Jacob has stolen Esau's birthright and his blessing.

Esau then shouts with a voice that carries out across the tent village, "I hate Jacob! I will kill my brother!" These are the last words we hear from Esau until the brothers meet years later. On hearing this threat, Jacob flees in fear. The brothers are bitter enemies.

For many years they live separately. They have families and become wealthy. When Jacob faces difficulties with his wives' brothers, he hears the Lord say, "Return to the land of your ancestors and to your kindred, and I will be with you" (31:3). He is to return to the land where Esau lives.

Now, after twenty years of grabbing and running, Jacob was coming home. Jacob turns his face toward Esau and the land of Seir. And he is afraid. As he progresses on his journey, he sends messengers with gifts to appease his brother. They return saying that Esau, hearing that Jacob is coming, has set out to meet him with four hundred men.

Jacob becomes greatly distressed. He cries out to God: "Deliver me from the hand of my brother, from the hand of Esau, for I am afraid of him. He may come and kill us all, the mothers with the children." (32:11, adapted) But Jacob continues the journey toward Esau, sending gifts ahead each day as he travels.

The night before Jacob meets Esau, he comes to a ford in the stream Jabbok. He sends his wives, children, and everything he has across the stream and stays behind, alone. During the night a man comes and wrestles with him until daybreak. When the man sees that he cannot overcome Jacob, he strikes Jacob's hip out of joint and demands to be let go. But Jacob will not let him go until he gives Jacob a blessing. The man then blesses him and gives him a new name, Israel. Jacob says, "I have seen the face of God, and yet my life is preserved." He names the place Peniel, "The face of God," so it will be remembered (32:22-30).

The next morning Jacob rises to meet Esau. After he crosses the stream, he sees Esau coming with four hundred men. He arranges his family behind him. Turning toward his brother, Jacob bows to the ground seven times as he approaches Esau. But Esau runs to meet him, embraces him, falls on his neck, and kisses him. And they weep (33:1-4).

"What do you mean by sending me all these things?" Esau asks.
"I wanted to find your favor," Jacob replies.
"I have enough," Esau declares.
"No, please; ... accept my present from my hand," Jacob says, " for truly to see your face is like seeing the face of God" (33:10).
Then after several days together, the brothers separate again. Each chooses a different valley, and they move apart.[2]

I have chosen this story because it has many similarities to this study. The wrong doer and the victim are from the same family. In our situation, the wrong doer and the victim were part of the same Church. Jacob and Esau's conflict lasted twenty years. Oppression in Lithuania lasted for fifty years. The victim Esau lost everything. The Lithuania Church after the Soviet occupation lost everything, the right to teach, the right to proclaim the gospel, as well as social influence and all property. Most importantly, many of the Church's sons died in Siberia or were killed. In both cases, the journey to reconciliation was a long one.

John Paul Lederach, in his book *The Journey Toward Reconciliation*, offers the following interpretation of the story:

It leads through a metaphorical moment, "I have seen the face of God."
It moves on to a powerful similitude, or point of comparison:

---

[2] See John Paul Lederach, *The Journey Toward Reconciliation* (Scottsdale, Pennsylvania: Herald Press, 1999), 17-21.

"to see your face is like seeing the face of God."

When we read such narratives in the Bible, we too often lose track of the genuine human qualities. We tend to see the stories as sacred and removed from our own reality. But look closely. We can see and feel the real human nature woven into the telling. What I find most intriguing are the parts left untold in the story. We must explore them in our search for understanding the process of reconciliation.

We find two brothers, one who tricks the other. We feel the depth of Esau's pain in the deception. He cries time and again for his father to bless him. His cry turns to bitter hatred. We see Jacob flee in fear. His deceptive actions will haunt him. The brothers move apart both physically and emotionally.

Here we ponder profound questions about conflict and reconciliation.

How and when do we surface and address the injustice that was committed? How and in what ways is putting distance between persons, moving apart, a necessary part of the journey toward reconciliation? How do we respond to people who are at this point in their journey? The pain is so deep, the injustice so clear and immediately present, and the emotions so high! Is it legitimate to separate?[3]

The questions that Lederach has raised in the last paragraph fit our situation in Lithuania. First of all, these are no quick formulae for forgiveness. From this story we can see that reconciliation is a long, long journey. Another very powerful image is presented about reconciliation: that reconciliation is seeing God's face in the face of the former wrong doers. Is this possible for human beings? From this story, it is very clear that reconciliation is possible but first of all it is God's work. The journey through conflict towards reconciliation always involves the person, as in this story Jacob, bringing fear to the situation because his brother was an enemy to him for 20 years. First, he has to deal with himself, his own fears, his own past; he has to prepare himself for the journey of reconciliation. On this journey he has to fight with the stranger. During that night, he fights with his own past and his own fears about the future. Then he sees the face of God.[4]

The journey towards reconciliation always includes people who did wrong to you, the wrongdoers. In the case of Jacob, he had to make two important changes in his journey: first, he turns toward Esau; second he seeks the face of his brother. Jacob

[3] John Paul Lederach, *The Journey Toward Reconciliation*, 19-20.
[4] Ibid., 23-25.

exclaims, "Seeing your face is like seeing the face of God." These are very powerful words, saying that reconciliation is the work of God.[5]

Paul Lederach mentions three important elements about reconciliation, and they are very much needed in our situation. First of all, reconciliation is the work of God; second, reconciliation should have a dialogue and a place; third, it is a journey, very dangerous and long, some times, which can only be accomplished by a later generation as in the Exodus story. God calls us to set out on this journey. It is a journey through conflict, marked by a place where we see the face of God, the face of the enemy, and the face of our own self.[6]

B. Jesus and His Teaching about Reconciliation

During interviews with former Lithuanian dissidents, mostly priests and religious people, I found that their knowledge of the theology of reconciliation was very limited. Sometimes when I asked about biblical texts, which supported the idea of reconciliation and forgiveness, dissidents for whom reconciliation was very difficult found the opposite of the normally accepted meaning of the passage. One of them said that even Jesus did not forgive the wrongdoer who did not repent. Why do we have to forgive those who persecuted us?

When the Nobel prize-winning South African Bishop Desmond Tutu read this Bible passage, he interpreted it quite differently:

> None of us could in my theology ever consign anyone to hell as being ultimately irredeemable. When Jesus was crucified it was in the company of two thieves. One of them became repentant and Jesus promised that he would be in paradise with him on that day. The thrust of that story is that not one of us could say with any certainty that so-and-so had gone to perdition, because none of us could ever know whether even the most notorious sinner and evildoer had not at the eleventh hour repented and been forgiven, because our God is preeminently the God of grace. What we are, what we have, even our salvation, all is gift, all is grace, not to be achieved but to be received as a gift freely given. God's bias in favor of sinners is so immense that it is said we will be surprised at those we will find in heaven whom we had not expected to encounter there.[7]

---

[5] Ibid., 22-23.
[6] John Paul Lederrach, *The Journey Toward Reconciliation*, 40-42.
[7] Desmond Mpilo Tutu, *No Future Without Forgiveness*, 86.

Theologian Miroslav Volf, in his article "The Meaning of Social Reconciliation," notes:

> One way to argue for the primacy of reconciliation in the New Testament would be to look at the Gospel accounts of the life of Jesus. This would lead us to highlight grace and forgiveness, which are so prominent in Jesus' encounters with 'the sinners' - grace and forgiveness, I hasten to add, that do not stand in opposition to justice and blame, but affirm justice and blame in the act of transcending them. Another way to argue for the primacy of reconciliation would be to examine the ethical appropriation of the basic story of Christ - his life, death and resurrection - in the New Testament writings. This would lead us to highlight the narrative of the death of Christ - the innocent victim - as the paradigm for the Christian life of self-donation. A third way to argue biblically for the primacy of reconciliation would be to concentrate directly on the theology of reconciliation developed by the Apostle Paul.[8]

We will examine the texts from the Gospels and Paul's letters that can speak to the Lithuanian Church's experiences in the post-communist world, where reconciliation within the Church and social reconciliation within society is needed.

Every person and every culture must read scripture within the Spirit of Christ. This cannot be done without listening carefully to Jesus, as he is presented in the New Testament. The gospel writers proclaim that he is the messianic bearer of the Spirit, announcing and embodying God's reign of justice and peace. Of particular interest to us here is Jesus' teachings about reconciliation and his actual conflict with the forces of injustice. Where reconciliation is concerned, the biblical material about Jesus does not present us with a simple or unambiguous picture. Jesus' life and teaching are characterized by a certain dialectic, for he holds together, on the one hand, a radical love of the enemy, and, on the other, forthright confrontation with the perpetrators of injustice. We distort the wisdom of his teaching if we neglect either of these.

The call to a radical love in the teaching of Jesus is extraordinary. When he is asked, "If your brother sins against you, how often should I forgive? As many as seven times?" Jesus said to him, "Not seven times, but, I tell you, seventy times seven." (Mt 18:21-22) For Jesus, reconciliation is more important than ritual: 'If you are offering

---

[8] Miroslav Volf, "The Social Meaning of Reconciliation" in *Journal of Religion in Eastern Europe*, Vol. XVIII (1998): 22-23.

your gift at the altar, and there remember that your brother has something against you, leave your gift before the altar and go first be reconciled to your brother, and then come and offer your gift!' (Mt 5:23)[9]

Followers of Jesus cannot evade the command about the love of enemies: "I say unto you, love your enemies, and pray for those who persecute you." (Mt 5:44) Jesus illustrates the love of enemies in his parable of the Good Samaritan, where an ethnic and religious "enemy" is the hero of the story. (Lk 10:29-37)[10] It is very similar to how the Lithuanian Church in resistance interpreted those who were thinking differently, they were thought of as ethnic and religion enemies. This was the way that all atheists were thought of. They were religious enemies because they were atheists. If one does not believe as we believe, then one is a foreigner and our enemy. It is different from the reaction of American leaders after the September 11, 2001 terrorist attacks when they clearly differentiated between the terrorists and the Islamic believers and Arabic nations. What happened in Samaria at the time of Jesus is very similar to what is happening in our times, but not in all situations do we react as Jesus reacted.

Harold Wells, in his article "Theology of Reconciliation," says:

> Jesus also praises a Roman centurion (Mt 8:5-10) and the Samaritan leper, "this foreigner," who alone returned to give thanks. (Lk 17:17) He offends the people of Nazareth when he suggests that God's blessing rests upon such foreigners as the widow of Zarephath in Sidon and Naaman the Syrian. (Lk 4:26-27) In all of this, Jesus' teaching stands as a sharp rebuke to all who call themselves Christian, attend worship, receive the sacraments, yet nurture in their hearts a hateful ethnicism, racism, or a feeling of religious superiority. It is sad that this attitude of Jesus about "others" has been so neglected in the teaching of the churches that Christians can engage in ethnic hatred, torture, and even genocide without realizing that they directly disobey their Lord.[11]

During the Sermon on Mount Jesus says, " Love your enemies and pray for those who persecute you, so that you may be children of your Father in heaven; for he

---

[9] Harold Wells, "Theology of Reconciliation" in Gregory Baum and Harold Wells (ed), *The Reconciliation of Peoples* (Maryknoll, New York: Orbis Books, 1997), 5-6.
[10] Ibid., 6.
[11] Ibid.

makes his sun rise on the evil and on the good, and sends rain on the righteous and on the unrighteous." (Mt 5:44-45) The incentive is the imitation of God. If we want to be like God, then we must act the way God acts: God forgives us, so we must forgive others. Jesus spells out what love of enemies might entail when he says: "You have heard that it was said, 'An eye for an eye and a tooth for a tooth.' But I say unto you, do not resist an evildoer. But if anyone strikes you on the right cheek, turn the other also." (Mt 5:39) In his article Harold Wells continues, "To love God and to love the neighbor as oneself is "the whole of the law and the prophets," (Mt 22:40) and this cannot be formulated into rigid principles. Those engaged in tragic and desperate struggles generally know that there are no simple rules or formulae for loving neighbors, or for achieving justice or reconciliation. Sometimes love of the enemy requires precisely that the enemy be effectively resisted."[12]

What must be seen together with Jesus' radical teaching about forgiveness and the love of enemies is that he does not flee from confrontation or gloss over painful conflict. He is severe indeed in his verbal attacks upon some religious leaders and teachers, whom he accuses in the most vivid terms of self-righteousness, hypocrisy, and injustice. He wields a whip of cords to cleanse the temple, which had become a "den of thieves." (Lk 19:46) He declared, "Do not think that I have come to bring peace on the earth. I have come not to bring peace, but a sword." (Mt 10:34) These are the words and deeds of one who aggressively confronts what he sees as evil. According to Luke, Jesus at one time instructed his disciples, "The one who has no sword must sell his cloak and buy one." (Lk 22:36) He is aware of the reality of conflict and struggle and of the necessity to resist evil actively.[13]

Harold Wells' article *"Theology of Reconciliation"* concludes:

> Unfortunately, very often the attitude of Jesus about forgiveness and his own unresisting way to the cross are emphasized to the exclusion of this other sharply confrontational dimension. To many of those engaged in fierce struggle, Jesus seems to be merely soft and passive, irrelevant to the urgency of the fight that must be fought. At the same time, his call to radical love and forgiveness has been simply ignored by Christians who engage in hateful and spiteful practices of revenge. Jesus was considered dangerous enough to be gotten rid of by the authorities. His enemies were never reconciled with him. He sought no false peace with those who oppressed the people. Yet he was able to

---

[12] Harold Wells, "Theology of Reconciliation," 6.
[13] Ibid., 5-6.

love them even as they tortured and executed him: "Father forgive them, for they do not know what they are doing." (Lk 23:34) These words are precious to us, for they have become an assurance of the breadth and depth of the divine mercy. Jesus' teaching and courageous example make us poignantly aware of our universal failure, indeed our own powerlessness to love, as we should, and to forgive as we should.[14]

a. The Resurrection Stories

The Resurrection stories can help us understand reconciliation more deeply. Especially in countries that were oppressed for a long period of time, the theology of the Paschal Mystery stopped at the events of Good Friday. Ash Wednesday and Good Friday celebrations were more significant and more important than the celebration of Easter Sunday. If we look at Jesus' images, we would find through history that the Lithuanian culture preferred a suffering God image. Before World War II, Professor Ignacijius Koncius researched Lithuanian religious folk art with his students by walking 2,224 kilometers and finding 3,234 folk religious sculptures. Almost half of them, 1,509, were crosses. The rest were statues of the "suffering Jesus" and 42% of the rest of the statues were of the sorrowful Mary, *pieta*. During this study, the image of the Risen Christ was not found among religious folk art.[15] Currently, in newly built church presbyteries, instead of the crucified Jesus, church designers are depicting the Risen Christ. Even though we are putting this image of Christ in our churches, the theology of what the resurrection says about reconciliation is not well known in Lithuania.

The resurrection stories help us to discover a Christian meaning to reconciliation. Those stories are powerful in shaping our identity. The stories of the suffering, death, and resurrection are central. I want to concentrate and to make some parallels using two stories: the empty tomb image, and one of the appearance stories, the Emmaus story.

The Gospel says that when the women approached the tomb of Jesus they did not find the body of Jesus. They had been witnesses to his crucifixion and very humiliating death on the cross. They were living in an occupied country and the State power was maintained by these fearsome feats of violence. Usually, the executed bodies were cut down from the cross and thrown into the garbage dump for the final

---

[14] Harold Wells, "Theology of Reconciliation," 7.

[15] J. Vaišnora, *Marijos Garbinimas Lietuvoje* (Roma: Lietuvių Katalikų Mokslo Akademija, 1958), 110.

humiliation. But the authorities allowed the followers of Jesus to bury him in a tomb. When the women on the next morning found the tomb empty, they thought that the body had "disappeared." The Gospel says that "they fled from the tomb, for terror and amazement had seized them; and they said nothing to anyone, for they were afraid." (Lk 16:8) John's Gospel says that only Mary Magdalene came to the tomb. Her words in John's Gospel, "They have taken away my Lord, and I do not know where they have laid him." (Jn 20:13) [16]

The empty tomb story and the women's concern that Jesus' body disappeared reminds us in part of Lithuanian history. After WWII, when the Soviets occupied Lithuania, a partisan movement followed. People resisted the Soviet regime in the partisan movement. When the Soviet military forces killed a partisan, they followed the same plan that the Roman occupiers did during Christ's time. They put the dead bodies in the main square of the town or city and put their guard near the bodies and did not allow the relatives of the deceased to bury them. And if someone looking at the bodies began to cry, he or she immediately became a suspect. Maybe he or she was a collaborator or maybe a relative of the deceased, a mother or sister. Those who cried were arrested and interrogated. If it was determined that they were relatives, they were deported to Siberia. After a few days the bodies were taken from the town square and then covered over in garbage dumps, gravel pits, or thrown into wells or latrines. [17] There are many similarities to what was done during Jesus' time. The grief of the relatives of the victims existed for long decades. A similar situation existed for those Lithuanians who were sent to Siberia. It was not allowed to bury their bodies in a traditional Russian cemetery. They were buried somewhere in an insignificant place where Lithuanians or other exiles were allowed to have their own cemeteries.

The first year of my priestly ministry was exactly the same period of time that Lithuania was becoming a free country. One of the first things that people did was rebury their loved ones. Those Lithuanians who were killed in Lithuania and buried in unconsecrated land were reburied during those three months. About 20,000 of those who died in Siberia were brought back to Lithuania for reburial. This first summer of my ministry I had from two to four funerals every day because I was the associate in the Cathedral. I had to bury those who died that year and perform rituals for those who had died in Siberia and those who were reburied in Lithuania. One of those funerals was that of my grandfather, who was brought from Siberia. This experience helped me

---

[16] Robert Schreiter, *The Ministry of Reconciliation: Spirituality and Strategies* (Maryknoll, NY: Orbis Books, 1998), 23-24.
[17] A. Ž., a.k.a. Spengla V., "LKB Kronikos ištakos, jos balsas Lietuvoje ir pasaulyje," Upublished Manuscript, 8.

understand these words: "They have taken away my Lord and I don't where they have laid him." (Jn 20:13)

The confusion and fear that the women experienced in Mark's Gospel and the disorientation of Mary Magdalene in John's Gospel reveal a tangled web of emotions and thoughts. The trauma of the execution of Jesus was still in their minds. The tomb was open and the body gone. It is like being thrown off balance by sifting sand. There is no orientation point to regain equilibrium. For the women, the tomb itself served as an anchor in the stormy seas of emotion that surrounded Jesus' violent death. The tomb was a place where the women could come and give focus to their feelings of loss, but now the tomb itself had been violated. The absence of the body from the tomb breaks again the relationship that burial tried to establish. Death is always a rupture of relationships, and grieving and mourning are a way of trying to reestablish relationships, albeit now in a different way. This is portrayed in a poignant fashion in John's account of Mary's recognizing that the stranger is Jesus. Jesus tells her not to cling to him: "Do not hold on to me." One cannot hold on to the dead; a new kind of relationship has to be established.[18]

The experience through which the women and the apostles went through in the crucifixion and death until the time when they recognized the risen Christ was very confusing, emotional, and depressing. I can here draw a parallel between this and the Lithuanian Church dissident group. The time of transition is the most difficult. For centuries the Church became familiar with resistance, first the Czars and then the Soviet regime. The times of transition towards reconstruction are very difficult, as one of the dissidents said. Earlier it was easier because we knew who our enemy was. Now we do not know whom we have to fight. This reminds us that the dissident acts like the apostles did after the death of Jesus, before they recognized the Risen Christ. The story of the empty tomb only takes us through the first part of the experience. They encounter profound absence- the descent among the dead and get only the slightest glimmer of what is to come. Now it is time to move to the story of Emmaus because the disciples on the Emmaus road are taken through an entirely new experience. As they make the journey out of Jerusalem to Emmaus, they journey also through disillusionment and disappointment.

_____

[18] Robert Schreiter, *The Ministry of Reconciliation: Spirituality and Strategies*, 32-35.

92

b. The Emmaus Story

During theological studies in Lithuania, this story was read from the perspective of proving the divinity of Jesus. During a thirty-day retreat, it was interpreted as a story, which invites people to individual sanctity. If you would be without sin, you would recognize Jesus on the road to Emmaus. There is another interpretation of this story, which says that this story reflects on the historical experience of the disciples. Let us interpret this story in terms of reconciliation. It shows how the gospels have multi-layered meanings. This story is one of the best stories in the Gospels.

In the Emmaus journey, the disciples say, "But we had hoped that He was the one to redeem Israel." That hope for the disciples is something from the past. The women's report of the empty tomb leaves them even more confused. The man who is accompanying them quoted them passage after passage from the writings of the prophets beginning with the book of Genesis and going right on to the scriptures explaining what the passages meant and what they said about Jesus. The words of the stranger have a significant impact on the disciples. When they were breaking bread, they recognized that this stranger is Jesus himself. This story reveals for us the meaning of the Resurrection and process and spirituality of reconciliation.[19]

The journey we make to reconciliation often seems like the disciples' journey to Emmaus. As one of the former dissidents said, "When nobody persecuted the Church, it was difficult to find what we have to do next. After long meditation and prayers, I found that we have to forgive our enemy."

Theologian Robert Schreiter, in his book *The Ministry of Reconciliation*, writes:

> "This is the experience of many who deal with a painful past. They can get all the words right, but something still is missing. It still does not all come together. In the Emmaus story in Luke, what was missing was faith. In our own struggle toward reconciliation, what is missing is often not that clear. We struggle to find the one thing that will help us overcome the pain, transform the memory, allow us to get on with our lives. But it just does not seem to come. The struggle to find the way to interpret our story is frequently a gradual retelling of that story until it become a new story."[20]

---

[19] Robert Schreiter, *The Ministry of Reconciliation: Spirituality and Strategies*, 41.
[20] Ibid., 43.

We just quoted an experience of a former dissident who sees Jesus in a new way, who sees a Risen Jesus; but for many of the dissidents, they find themselves stuck and unable to maneuver in a new situation. And because they were not able to maneuver, they became frustrated with their friend's new approach to reconciliation, that of supporting communist people. They acted in a way to which they had become accustomed. They collected a petition against their former friend and printed their denunciation of him in the press. Of course, during the Soviet occupation when they were condemning the Soviet regime, these same types of documents were read on Voice of America and Vatican Radio. It made an impact. Now those petitions are not significant and make some people laugh. But it shows that this group is still on a journey, in which they cannot see the Risen Jesus or see the situation in a new light. They repeat the same formula, they tell the same stories, but nothing ever changes and the burden never becomes lighter. They are interpreting that something wrong is happening in society but they cannot retell their own dissident story in a new light. They cannot place their own story in the bigger story of the passion, death, and resurrection of Jesus. The Emmaus story contains the main elements of spirituality and the ministry of reconciliation. This is probably why it is one of the favorite stories of the Gospels.

c. Pauline Text on Reconciliation

Now let us consider Paul's theology of reconciliation and focus upon a key Pauline text on reconciliation, 2 Corinthians 5:17-21, and explore the social dimension of reconciliation in Paul's theology,[21] Paul writes:

> So if anyone is in Christ, there is a new creation: everything old has passed away; see, everything has become new! All this is from God, who reconciled us to himself through Christ, and has given us the ministry of reconciliation that is in Christ God was reconciling the world to himself, not counting their trespasses against them, and entrusting the message of reconciliation to us. So we are ambassadors for Christ, since God is making his appeal through us; we entreat you on behalf of Christ, be reconciled to God. For our sake he made him to be sin who knew no sin, so that in him we might become the righteousness of God. (2 Cor 5:17-21)

---

[21] Robert Schreiter, *The Ministry of Reconciliation: Spirituality and Strategies*, 50-51.

We chose 2 Corinthians 5:17-21 because it has a lot to say about the situation in the Lithuanian Catholic Church today. Actually the meaning of this text is usually ignored. The second reason for choosing this text is that it shows the Catholic approach towards reconciliation. As Robert Schreiter argues, "The Catholic emphasis would be slightly different (compared with that of Protestant), focusing on the love of God poured out upon us as a result of the reconciliation God has effected in Christ. Here the emphasis is on the new creation. If there is a classic location for this theology, it is 2 Corinthians 5:17-20."[22]

Seyoon Kim says: "Paul never says that God is reconciled (or, that God reconciles himself) to human beings, but always that God reconciles human beings to himself or that human beings are reconciled to God. It is not, in fact, God who must be reconciled to human beings, but human beings need to be reconciled to God. Nor is it by people' s repentance, prayers or other good works that reconciliation between God and human beings is accomplished, but rather by God's grace alone."[23]

What Kim notes here about God (the offended -victim party) offering reconciliation to humanity, the offender-victim is now the standard explanation of the passage. What is new in Kim's argument is his account of how Paul came to this unique understanding of reconciliation. He argues persuasively that the origin of Paul's distinct use of the term reconciliation lies in Paul's encounter with the risen Christ on the road to Damascus where he was headed to persecute the early followers of Jesus Christ. Kim concludes, "It is most likely that Paul's use of the metaphor of reconciliation grew out of his own theological reflections on his Damascus road conversion experience. This thesis explains, more plausibly than any other, the fundamental innovation that Paul made in the idea of reconciliation that is, that it is not human beings who reconcile an angry God to themselves rather, it is God who reconciles human beings to himself through the atoning death of Jesus Christ. For on the Damascus road, Paul, who came to see himself as God's enemy in his activities before Damascus, experienced God's reconciling action, which brought forgiveness of sins and the making of a new creation by his grace."[24]

---

[22] Robert Schreiter, *The Ministry of Reconciliation: Spirituality and Strategies*, 14.
[23] Seyoon Kim, "God Reconciled His Enemy to Himself: The Origins of Paul's Concept of Reconciliation," in R. N. Longnecker (ed), *The Road from Damascus* (Grand Rapids: Eerdmans, 1997), 103.
[24] Miroslav Volf, "The Social Meaning of Reconciliation" in *Journal of Religion in Eastern Europe*, Vol XVIII (1998): 24.

In his article "The Social Meaning of Reconciliation" Miroslav Volf notes:

> Two significant features of a theology of reconciliation emerge with clarity, features of great import for the proper understanding of its social meaning. First, *though grace is unthinkable without justice, justice is subordinate to grace.* As a persecutor of the Church, Paul was an enemy of God (or, more precisely, he came to see himself in retrospect as an enemy of God). In conversion, Paul encountered God who was not wrathful, as God should have been, but who instead showed love by offering to reconcile Paul, the enemy, to himself. Paul's conversion was not the result of the pursuit of strict justice on the part of the "victim." Had the "victim" pursued strict justice, Paul never would have become the apostle of the very Church he was persecuting. [25]

Inscribed in the narrative of the very event that transformed him from persecutor to apostle was the message which Paul came to proclaim the message that God *justifies the ungodly* (Romans 4:5), that we were reconciled to God *while we were enemies* (Romans 5: 10). At the core of the doctrine of reconciliation lies the belief that the offer of reconciliation is not based on justice done and the cause of enmity removed. Rather, the offer of reconciliation is a way of justifying the unjust and overcoming the opponents' enmity, not so as to condone their injustice and affirm their enmity, but to open up the possibility of doing justice and living in a peace whose ultimate shape is a community of love. [26]

Paul was saved through the divine grace by which God sought to reconcile the enemy, which closes its eyes before injustice. That happened on the road to Damascus. The divine voice named the action by its proper name - "persecution" - and asked the uncomfortable "why?" "Saul, Saul, why do you persecute me?" (Acts 9:4). Jesus Christ himself named the injustice and made the accusation in the very act of offering forgiveness and reconciliation. Divine justice was an indispensable element of reconciliation, reconciliation was not simply the consequence of divine justices carried out. [27]

---

[25] Ibid., 27.

[26] Miroslav Volf, "The Social Meaning of Reconciliation" in *Journal Religion of Religion in Eastern Europe*, Vol XVIII (1998): 27.

[27] Ibid., 27-28.

In his article *The Social Meaning of Reconciliation* Miroslav Volf continues to analyze Paul's theology of reconciliation:

> "Second, though *reconciliation of human beings to God has priority, reconciliation between human beings is intrinsic to their reconciliation to God.* The origin of Paul's message of reconciliation was his encounter with the risen Christ on the road to Damascus. The enmity toward God results in enmity toward other human beings. God does not hold against us our human trespasses because of the atoning death of Christ. In the account in Acts we read that "Saul was ravaging the Church by entering house after house; dragging off both men and women, he committed them to prison" (Acts 8:3). On the road to Damascus, he was "still breathing threats and murder against the disciples of the Lord" (9: 1). At the same time, the voice from heaven identified itself explicitly as the voice of Jesus Christ: "I am Jesus, whom you are persecuting" (9:4-5). So from the start and at its heart, the enmity toward God is enmity toward human beings, and the enmity toward human beings is enmity toward God. Consequently, from the start, reconciliation does not simply have a vertical but also a horizontal dimension. It contains a turn away from the enmity toward people, not just from enmity to God, and it contains a movement toward a community, precisely that community which was the target of enmity. Just as the 'persecutor was received by God in Christ, so the persecutor was received by the community which he had persecuted. And he in turn sought to give a gift to the community that received him: he became a builder of the very community that he sought to destroy (Acts 9:20)."[28]

Paul argued that the pattern of the divine reconciling movement toward estranged humanity is the model of how the followers of Christ should relate to their enemies, whether they are Christians or not (Romans 15:7). Hence it is no accident that in the circle around Paul a grand vision of reconciliation was conceived: "For in him (Christ) all the fullness of God was pleased to dwell, and through him God was pleased to reconcile to himself all things, whether on earth or in heaven, by making peace through the blood of his cross" (Colossians 1:20). The ultimate vision not only for the Church but also for the whole of reality is a vision of the reconciliation of all

---

[28] Miroslav Volf, "The Social Meaning of Reconciliation" in *Journal of Religion in Eastern Europe*, Vol XVIII (1998): 28.

things.[29]

The Pauline vision of reconciliation is a vision that entails a coherent set of fundamental beliefs about the nature of God and of human beings and about the relation between justice and love--lies at the core of the Christian faith. If social engagement is to be properly Christian, it must to be governed by this vision. And only if social engagement is governed by this vision do churches have adequate theological resources to resist the temptation to become accomplices in conflicts and instead function as agents of peace.

Robert Schreiter summarizes Paul's teaching on reconciliation in five points:
1. **Reconciliation is the work of God, who initiates and completes in us reconciliation through Christ.**
2. **Reconciliation is more spirituality than a strategy.**
3. **The experience of reconciliation makes of both victim and wrongdoer a new creation.**
4. **The process of reconciliation that creates the new humanity is to be found in the story of the passion, death, and resurrection of Jesus Christ.**
5. **The process of reconciliation will be fulfilled only with the complete consummation of the world by God in Christ.**[30]

I think that the one major reason why the Lithuanian Catholic Church still is living in the spirit of resistance is that the Church does not have adequate theological resources to resist the temptation to be in conflict. It is especially clear that the part of the Church which was involved in the resistance is still struggling with resistance. It is exactly as Robert Schreiter says: "First and foremost, the reconciliation that Christians have to offer in overcoming the enmity created by suffering is not something they find in themselves, but something they recognize as coming from God. Thus the question is not how can I bring myself, as victim, to forgive those who have violated me and my society? It is, rather, how can I discover the mercy of God welling up in my own life, and where does that lead me? Reconciliation, then, is not a process that we initiate or achieve. We discover it already active in God through Christ... God takes the initiative, that reconciliation is something that we discover rather than achieve."[31]

The collapse of Communist domination in countries of Eastern Europe raises a host of questions about a new order. In most of those countries the Church cannot

---

[29] Ibid., 32-34.
[30] Robert Schreiter, *The Ministry of Reconciliation: Spirituality and Strategies*, 14-19.
[31] Robert Schreiter, *Reconciliation: Mission and Ministry in a Changing Social Order* (Maryknoll, NY: Orbis Books, 1992), 43-44.

escape the question of reconciliation because the fault-line of violence runs right through the Church itself. In Czechoslovakia and Hungary, for example, what will be done with those Roman Catholic priests who were part of the so-called peace groups, officially sanctioned by a Communist regime that was at the same time imprisoning other Roman Catholics? How shall they relate to those who suffered imprisonment and other violence for their commitments to the Roman Catholic Church? Can they be reconciled to each other?[32]

The Lithuanian Church is in the same situation as the Czechoslovakian and Hungarian Church where still there is division between the so-called "loyal" and those who suffered imprisonment. If the Church wants to move toward reconciliation, then the Church has to learn reconciliation theology, not only to learn but to live as Christ said.

Of course there is no way to "forgive" the Nazis for what they did; or Stalin, for the murder of twenty million of his own people; or Pol Pot, for the slaughter of as much as a third of all Cambodians. Judgment for such horrendous crimes belongs to a tribunal much higher than any we might convene. Christians, however, are confronted in such cases not with the limits of our feelings (Is it possible for us to forgive?), but with the nature of the God revealed by Jesus. "For God makes the sun rise on the evil and on the good, and sends rain on the righteous and on the unrighteous.... Be all-inclusive in your love, as your heavenly Father is all-inclusive." (Matt 5:45, 48) In short, God is incapable of not forgiving, because it is God's very nature to forgive.[33]

One chapter in Desmond Tutu's book *No Future without Forgiveness* is concluded in a similar way: "A rustic Russian priest was accosted by a brash young physicist who rehearsed all the reasons for atheism and arrogantly went on, 'Therefore I do not believe in God.' The little priest, not put off at all, replied quietly, 'Oh, it doesn't matter. God believes in you.' God believes in us. God depends on us to help make this world all that God wants it to be."[34]

C. Reconciliation and Church Tradition

Within its two thousand years of history, the Church many times had to deal with persecution and oppression. When the atrocities stopped, Christians had to go through the process of reconciliation. There were some success stories and some failures.

---

[32] Ibid., 13.
[33] Walter Wink, *When the Powers Fall* (Minneapolis: Fortress Press, 1998), 17.
[34] Desmond Mpilo Tutu, *No Future Without Forgiveness*, 159.

a. Donatists

From the very beginning of Christianity, there were many situations where the Church was persecuted by governments. Governments attempted to use the Church as their own tool to reach their own goals. They tried to force Christians to collaborate with them, compromising their own beliefs. In many cases, this caused great divisions in the Church. The Church became divided between those who compromised and those who refused to collaborate. Times became very difficult when the oppressor suddenly was gone. Then the Church had to deal within its own community with those issues. What does one do with collaborators and how does one reconcile? One of the first well-known cases in Church history took place in North Africa when, after the Diocletian persecution, the Church was given freedom by the Emperor Constantine. The Church became divided around an issue of what to do with "traditores." In Church history it is known as the Donatist movement.

The Donatist movement originated in North Africa from the fourth to the seventh centuries. Mensurius, bishop of Carthage, cooperated with the Roman authorities during the Diocletian persecutions of the early fourth century. The Roman authorities were friendly and allowed him to give them heretical books to be burned rather than copies of Scriptural books.[35] He, in turn, agreed to suspend public worship services, hoping to lie low until the persecution died away. More radical Christians, called "confessores," who found themselves in prison for refusing any measure of cooperation with the authorities, denounced Mensurius as a "traditore" or betrayer for his cowardice. Mensurius' archdeacon Caecilian was so offended by their attacks that in AD 304 he picketed the local prison to prevent food being taken to the confessors.[36]

When Mensurius died in 311, Caecilian was quickly consecrated bishop by the urban Carthaginian bishops without waiting for the provincial bishops to arrive. It was alleged that bishop Felix, one of the consecrators, had been a "traditore" during the persecution under Diocletian. He had surrendered actual books of the consecrations and the Bible, and had been a "traitor" during the persecution under Diocletian. Both bishops Felix and newly ordained Caecilian was immediately rejected by the "confessores."[37] They believed a sinful bishop or priest could not validly administer the sacraments such as baptism, marriage, or the Eucharist. In this particular case, Caecilian was accused of being a "traditore." One who handed over his Bible to be

---

[35] *New Catholic Encyclopedia*, s.v. "Donatists."
[36] *The Catholic Encyclopedia*, s.v. "Donatists."
[37] John Anthony Corcoran , *Augustinus Contra Donatistas* (Donaldson, Indiana: Graduate Theological Foundation, 1997) 23-26.

destroyed. Holding that no "traditore" should be consecrated, a group of 70 dissident bishops – the nucleus of what would become the Donatist fraction – met and declared bishop Caecilian to be excommunicated and replaced him with another man, who was followed in turn by Donatus himself four years later.[38]

The Donatists believed that the presence of the Holy Spirit in a priest depended on his being in a state of grace himself. Clergy who were not virtuous as the "traditores" were the most obvious examples of those who had lost God's grace and could not properly baptize babies, turn bread and wine into the body and blood of Christ in the sacrament of Holy Communion, or ordain other clergy. Since everyone's salvation depended on receiving God's grace through baptism and Holy Communion, Donatists had to make sure that each of their priests was in a state of grace, and had been properly ordained by bishops who were also in a state of grace. Neither unworthy priests, nor priests whose ordination had failed because it had been performed by an unworthy bishop, could give the people the sacraments on which their salvation depended.[39]

"Confessores" appealed to the emperor Constantine to mediate the dispute and he, in turn, asked Pope Melchiades (311–314) to appoint three Gallic bishops to hear the case and to report to him. Pope Melchiades added fifteen Italian bishops and transformed it into a synod, meeting at the Lateran Palace. On October 3, 313, the synod rendered a verdict in favor of Caecilian, and excommunicated Donatus for having required the rebaptism of laypersons and the reordination of clergy who had compromised their faith during the Diocletian persecution. At the same time, pope Melchiades offered full communion to other North African bishops, allowing them to retain their episcopal sees. The Donatists were bitterly resentful of the verdict and began to spread rumors about Melchiades's own behavior during the persecution. They appealed once again to Constantine, who summoned a council of representatives from all the Western provinces to meet at Arles in August of 314. But this council confirmed the findings of The Council of Lateran Palace (313) and recognized the validity of the election of Caecilian of Cartagin, and confirmed the excommunication of Donatus.[40] It was the first time in which imperial authority was asked to uphold one Christian group and suppress another.[41]

Donatism was essentially a response to alternating periods of persecution followed by toleration, culminating in the beginning of the fourth century by the formal legalization of Christianity by Constantine. During Donatus' lifetime,

---

[38] *Encyclopedia of Heresies and Heretics*, s.v. "Donatism."
[39] Richard P. McBrien, *Catholicism* (Minneapolis: Winston Press, 1966), 751.
[40] Richard P. McBrien, *Lives of the Popes* (San Francisco: Harper & Row, 2000), 56-57.
[41] *Encyclopedia of Heresies and Heretics*, s.v. "Donatism."

Donatism became the dominant Christian Church in North Africa, but its fortunes declined by the third generation. Late in the fourth century and early in the fifth Catholic Christianity found formidable leadership in St. Augustine, who spent a good bit of his episcopate addressing the problem of Donatism.[42] At Augustine's death, both Catholic Christians and Donatist Christians suffered under the rule of the Vandal invaders, probably encouraging them to accept one another more easily. Though Donatism did flourish again in the sixth century, the entire North African Church was weakened and compromised by the internecine fighting, and proved unable to withstand the attractions of Islam in the seventh century, when the Christian Church disappeared entirely from western North Africa.[43]

In this situation no one thought about the process of reconciliation. It is for these reasons Donatists required justice and truth; but in the process of reconciliation, these elements should be taken into account: peace, mercy and, forgiveness. Another reason that reconciliation did not happen was that the conflict took place at the beginning of the authoritarian Church. During this conflict, the Emperor Constantine and the Popes supported not the former oppressed group, the "confessors," but those who collaborated, the "traditores." Part of the reason was that the Donatists were supported by small town churches and bishops. The Emperor and the Popes identified with the big cities: Rome and Carthage.[44] Pope Marcelinus (296-304) during the Diocletian persecution complied with imperial orders to hand over copies of Sacred Scriptures and to offer incense to the gods. Such individuals were known as "traditores." Three future popes, Marcellus (306-308), Melchiades (311-314), and Sylvester were his clergy during his papacy.[45]

This case demonstrates as well how soon the oppressed can become the oppressor. The Donatists in North Africa became the oppressors to the Christians who did not accept their teachings. St. Augustine thought that the best way to deal with schismatics was to send an army to their city.[46] The history of the Church during this period shows that the clergy who had been the oppressed when they became free by Constantine's decree became the oppressors of the non-Christian population. During the time of the Constantine Church there was no place for the Theology of Reconciliation. We can see this during medieval times, reformation and colonization. It is only in the 20th century that the Theology of Reconciliation found a place in the practice of the Church.

---

[42] John Anthony Corcoran, *Augustinus Contra Donatistas,* 71-86.
[43] *The Catholic Encyclopedia,* s.v. "Donatism."
[44] John Anthony Corcoran, *Augustinus Contra Donatistas,* 17-37.
[45] Richard P. McBrien, *Lives of the Popes,* 54.
[46] John Anthony Corcoran, *Augustinus Contra Donatistas,* 110-112.

b. France

Another case from recent Church history in which the Church had to deal with the wrongdoer issue was with the French Catholic Church after World War II. When the Nazi government fell, France was liberated and the Church enjoyed freedom again. The future Pope John XXIII, as Nuncio Roncalli, had to deal with the very delicate issue of the Church officials who had collaborated with the Vichy regime.

The legitimacy and popularity of the Vichy government was relatively widespread at first, partly because it kept France out of World War II and maintained the existence of the French Empire. General Charles de Gaulle established an opposition movement in exile, but relatively few left France to join. A variety of anti-Vichy resistance groups did gradually organize within France, culminating in the establishment of the umbrella *Counseil National de la Resistance* (CNR). On June 3, 1943, General de Gaulle formed the *Comite Francais de Liberation National*, which then became the Provisional Government of the French Republic. France was liberated in December 1944. The punishment of those who collaborated with the Vichy government began.[47]

One of those suspected was no less than Cardinal Suhard, Archbishop of Paris, who had taken up his office in 1940 at the very time of the debacle. When Paris was liberated General de Gaulle attended a famous Te Deum in Notre Dame, but Suhard was not allowed in his own cathedral; he was ordered to remain in his residence. This rebuff was due to Cardinal Suhard's effusive welcoming of Petain to Paris as late as April, 1944, and, to a greater extent perhaps, due to Suhard's conducting a service for the deceased pro-Nazi propagandist Philippe Henriot. De Gaulle also refused to recognize Msgr. Valeri as nuncio because of his collaboration with the Vichy regime. Leon Berard, Vichy's representative at the Holy See, was kept under virtual house arrest at the Vatican. Valeri was replaced by Roncalli in January, 1945. Jacques Maritain was sent to the Vatican as the French ambassador. A number of bishops fell into government disfavor because of their support of Vichy. Local prefects arrested the Bishops of Arras and of Saint-Brieu.[48]

One of the best studies about this situation is W.D. Halls' book *Politics, Society and Christianity in Vichy France*. In his exploration of the early days of Vichy, Halls focuses on the attitudes and actions of the Catholic episcopacy, which

---

[47] Neil J. Kritz, *Transitional Justice* (Washington, DC: United States Institute of Peace Press, Vol. 2, 1995): 71.

[48] Harry W. Paul, *The Second Relliement: The Rapprochement Between Church and State in France in the Twentieth Century* (Washington, DC: The Catholic University of America Press, 1967), 182.

had little choice but to rally to Petain if it hoped to improve the relationship between the Church and the government. Many bishops anticipated Vichy support for parochial rather than lay education, and even hoped for the restitution of Church property confiscated in connection with the separation of Church and State in 1905. Halls finds evidence of Catholic clerics dreaming of a new Concordat for France. In all these aspirations, Catholic leaders would be sorely disappointed in Petain's cautious moves. Perhaps the only real compensation to the Church for backing the Vichy regime was escape from the threat of Nazification. Halls characterizes the Catholic Church hierarchy in 1940 as old and out of tune with the French population, but members of an age and experience cohort with Marshal Philippe Petain. Operating on conservative political premises, the Catholic leadership did little to criticize Hitler even in the pre-war period.[49]

One of the most valuable contributions of Halls' study is its presentation of detailed information about the activities of the Catholic bishops in a single volume, including an excellent appendix that identifies them by province and diocese. Here Halls brings nuance to his assessment of the attitudes and acts of individuals, instead of tarring all the Catholic hierarchy with a single brush. He recognizes that Pierre Cardinal Gerlier of Lyon remained staunchly Petainist, yet cites the lawyer and hunter of war criminals, Serge Klarsfeld's report that Gerlier also aided in curbing cooperation between the French police and the SS. The bishop of Beauvais, Monsignor Roeder, made a dramatic gesture when he appeared in full pontificals, preceded by an acolyte bearing a crucifix, to register for the German-mandated Jewish census, because one of his ancestors was Jewish. Monsignor Paul Remond, bishop of Nice, forbade the French anti-Jewish police to verify baptismal certificates from his diocese. Emmanuel Cardinal Suhard of Paris supported the German war effort to the very end, in large part because of his hatred for the Soviet Union. Still, Suhard frequently intervened to alleviate some of the worst German abuses. Halls' assessment of Monsignors Pierre-Marie Theas of Montauban and Jules-Gerard Saliege of Toulouse enhances their standing among a handful of the higher clergy who followed their consciences and stood up to the occupiers and their own government. If Halls accuses only two Catholic bishops of outright collaboration with the Nazis (many with Vichy, the rector of the Paris *Institut Catholique*, and the bishop of Arras) only a few members of the episcopacy had much reason to be proud.[50]

As early as July 26, 1944, the Interior Ministry had drawn up a list of bishops "who had caused the greatest scandal during the occupation." The list had twenty-five

---

[49] W. D. Halls, *Politics, Society and Christianity in Vichy, France* (Oxford: Berg Publisher, 1995), 15-31.
[50] Ibid., 341-379.

names, included three cardinals: Suhard (Paris), Gerlier (Lyons) and Lienart (Lille). Among these bishops was Beaussart, auxiliary of Paris and Courbe, head of Catholic Action. Later this number came to thirty. The government's efforts to obtain the replacement of thirty episcopal supporters of Vichy at the beginning found little cooperation at Rome.[51]

Later, the Vatican had to remove some of the bishops who had collaborated. But only three of them were removed officially. Others were "promoted" to higher positions in the Vatican and moved to Rome. Others had to retire for "health" reasons.[52] Collaboration with the Vichy and the Nazi regimes was one of the reasons why the Roman Catholic Church in France lost the working class.

We can see here an entirely different approach as to how the Church dealt with collaborators of the Nazi regime and how the Church is dealing with those who collaborated with the Soviet regime. The bishops who collaborated with the Vichy regime were removed. This is rarely done in Vatican practice. It was done because of pressure brought by the French government. The pressure resulted from the fact that the Church had not done everything possible to resist the Nazi regime. When the communist regime fell, in many countries the Church helped democratic governments and in many cases played a role in the liberation movements. When countries became free, in the minds of the people, the Church had many credits, having fought against the former regimes. The Vatican was excited about the victory against communism. The new governments did not have strength and knowledge, as had General DeGaulle, in how to deal with bishops and Church leaders who had collaborated with the Soviet regime. There are cases where bishops who were former collaborators remain in office even 10 years after independence. Ten years later, when the euphoria of the defeat of communism is gone, it is possible to see the negative effect of the Vatican not removing collaborators. Halls in his book notes: " such a purge was probably unnecessary. The Church, having adopted a subservient attitude to Vichy, would knuckle under to the new government in the same way. Had not this already proved to the case with the North African bishops?"[53] He had here in mind the Donatist movement and the North African bishops under the government of Emperor Constantine.

---

[51] Ibid., 352-361.
[52] John C. Dwyer, *Church History* (New York: Paulist Press, 1998), 385.
[53] W. D. Halls, *Politics, Society and Christianity in Vichy France*, 370.

c. Argentina

The armed forces seized power in Argentina in a 1976 coup d'etat that removed President Isabel Peron. The military coup was initially welcomed by much of society for ending a chaotic period characterized by widespread political violence and for replacing runaway inflation with apparent economic stability. However, the military junta unleashed a vicious campaign that came to be known as the "dirty war" for its brutality and continued it long after the elimination of any armed threat from the left, persecuting all "subversives" suspected of opposing the junta's virulently anti-Communist notion of Western Christian civilization. Torture was inflicted on a massive scale. In 1977 the Argentine commission for Human Rights, in Geneva, blamed the regime for 2,300 political murders. While refusing to acknowledge most arrests and detentions, the armed forces were suspected of causing to disappear and killing an estimated 10,000-30,000 people. Censorship and manipulation of press propaganda exaggerated the subversive threat while masking or denying governmental repression.[54]

Over time, international condemnation of the human rights abuses of the regime increased from the United Nations, foreign governments, and non-governmental organizations. Opposition also became more vocal within Argentina as a result of economic crises and growing domestic awareness of the abuses. In one prominent example, the "Mothers of the Plaza de Mayo"- mothers of disappeared people demanding information on the whereabouts and fate of their children-held weekly demonstrations in Buenos Aires' main square. Ultimately, the disgrace of military defeat in a 1982 war with Great Britain over the disputed Malvinas/Falklands islands forced the military to prepare for a return to civilian rule.[55]

With unprecedented international debt, and inflation at more than 900 percent, the military junta fell from power in disgrace in 1983. Following generally free elections, Raul Alfonsin was inaugurated in December 1983 as president. At the beginning, the civil government tried to tell the truth and was seeking justice. Within his first week in office, Alfonsin appointed a National Commission on Disappeared Persons under the leadership of the distinguished Argentine author, Ernesto Sabato. The Commission's final report, *Nunca Mas* ("Never Again"), was widely read in Argentina and abroad and provided powerful documentation of the systematic violation of human rights by the military regime. The "Law of National Pacification," an amnesty which the military granted itself before leaving office, was quickly repealed. The new government undertook prosecution of members of the first three

---

[54] Neil J. Kritz, *Transitional Justice*, Vol. 2 (1995): 323.
[55] Ibid.

juntas of the dictatorship for violations of human rights and mishandling of the Malvinas War. The armed forces were reorganized: former military and political leaders were charged with human right abuses. The military leaders were charged with over 700 separate crimes.[56]

A major tactical error, however, slowed the legal process to a crawl: the decision in 1984 to allow military courts to deal with their own and then, if the military courts failed to act responsibly, to involve the civil courts. Predictably, the military courts dawdled, equivocated, evaded, and finally sank into a mire of inactivity. Months, years passed. Meanwhile, the solidarity of civilians against the military gave way to factional politics in the style so celebrated in Argentina, while the military came together as a solid phalanx bitterly opposed to all prosecution. Four times, military officers staged attempted coups.[57] Still facing the prospect of numerous trials, junior army officers carried out a major rebellion during Easter week, 1987. Alfonsin met with the rebels and claimed to have resolved the crisis with no concessions, but within a few weeks he proposed to Congress the "Due Obedience Law" which was adopted in June. By creating an irrefutable presumption that all but the most senior military officers had only committed abuses under orders from their superiors, the law exonerated virtually all military personnel.[58]

Declaring that "permanent reconciliation among all Argentineans ... is the only possible solution for the wounds that still remain to be healed," President Carlos Menem, Alfonsin's successor, granted pardons in 1989 for 39 military officials convicted of or charged with human rights abuses, along with more than 200 other pardons for leftist guerillas, military personnel charged in connection with the Malvinas war, and those convicted for the mutinies under Alfonsin. In December 1990, Menem pardoned the convicted leaders of the junta.[59]

Walter Wink criticized the process of reconciliation in Argentina in these words: "amnesty should come only at the end of a reconciliation process, when the truth has been told, representative agents held accountable, and a process of healing catharsis has been allowed to run its course. The military has prevented that process of reconciliation from occurring."[60]

Only in January of 1992 was a law passed, which provided financial compensation to those who were jailed under the military regime, to relatives of political prisoners who had died in custody, and to those who were forced into exile

[56] Ibid., 323.
[57] Walter Wink, *When the Powers Fall* (Minneapolis: Fortress Press, 1998), 44.
[58] Neil J. Kritz, *Transitional Justice*, Vol. 2 (1995), 324.
[59] Ibid., 324.
[60] Walter Wink, *When the Powers Fall*, 45-46.

during the 1976-83 period.[61]

In Argentina, sadly, the Roman Catholic hierarchy was solidly on the side of military repression. Prominent Catholic bishops were fully informed of the plans to overthrow constitutional rule and set up a long-term military dictatorship that would lead to a new political and social order. The night before the change was announced, two of the coup leaders, General Jorge Videla and Admiral Emilio Massera, met with members of the hierarchy at the headquarters of the bishops' conference. The very day of the coup, March 24, 1976, members of the military junta met for a long time with Archbishop Adolfo Tortolo of Parana, who was the military vicar and president of the Bishops' Conference of Argentina.[62] The subsequent course of events revealed what kind of agreement they had made. The regime would get a green light for its repression and would enjoy the support of the episcopacy, in exchange for taking on the defense of "Western Christian civilization" and bolstering the privileges of the Church.[63]

The Argentine episcopacy was made up of more than eighty bishops, including heads of dioceses, auxiliary bishops, and military bishops. Only four of them took a stand of open denunciation of the human rights violations committed by the terrorist regime: Enrique Angelelli of La Rioja, who was murdered by the armed forces in what was made to look like a traffic accident on August 4, 1976; Jaime de Nevares of Neuquon; Miguel Hesayne of Viedma, who joined the Permanent Assembly for Human Rights; and Jorge Novak of Quilmes, who was made a bishop on September 19, 1976, and who joined the Ecumenical Movement for Human Rights.[64]

Within the framework of the military vicariate, chaplains to the military, the police, and the prisons - who were operationally under the control of the armed forces-cooperated with tortures. Much of the testimony presented to the courts and the National Commission on Disappeared Persons makes this clear. It stands in sharp contrast to the contemporary teaching and doctrine of the Catholic magisterium, as expressed by recent popes. In 1982 bishop Jose Miguel Medina was assigned to the military vicariate. The same year Bishop Medina stated, "Sometimes physical repression is necessary; it is obligatory, and thus licit."[65] In other words, torture is justifiable.

In *Nunca Mas* ("Never Again"), a report issued by the National Commission on Disappeared Persons, there is a transcription of part of a statement by Ernesto

---

[61] Neil J. Kritz, *Transitional Justice*, Vol. 2 (1995): 324.

[62] Emilio F. Mignone, *Witness to the Truth* (Maryknoll, New York: Orbis Books, 1988), 19.

[63] Emilio F. Mignone, *Witness to the Truth,* 19.

[64] Ibid., 19.

[65] Ibid., 10.

Reynaldo Saman (file 4841), which reads: "When I was in the prison in Villa Gorriti, Jujuy, Bishop Medina said Mass, and in the sermon he said that he knew what we were going through, but that all this was for the good of the country, and the military were working for good and we ought to tell everything we knew. For that purpose, he offered to hear confessions."[66]

Reverend Astigueta, air force chaplain in Cordoba, heard the confessions of prisoners before they were secretly shot to death. He never made a public denunciation, as he should have by law.[67] Reverend Gallardo, chaplain to the III Army Corps, also at Cordoba, used to visit the secret detention center in La Perla. He once told former congressional representative Musa, when he was being held there, that it was a sin to torture only if it lasted more than forty-eight hours.[68]

Catholic military chaplains actually blessed the murder of "subversives" as a necessity for preserving "Christian civilization." The preferred method of execution was drugging the victims and dropping them naked from thirteen thousand feet into the Atlantic Ocean.

Scilingo, a 28-year-old lieutenant, was stationed in Buenos Aires at the Naval School of Mechanics in 1977. He estimates that between 1,500 and 2,000 people "disappeared" in this manner from his base alone. He admits responsibility for 30 of them. He says he was ordered to participate in two of the death flights in 1977, adding that his fellow officers drew the same sort of assignment: "It was to give everyone a turn, a kind of Communion." On his first flight, Scilingo helped strip and then throw 13 victims out of a coast guard Sky Van; on his second, he did the same to 17 more out of a navy Elektra.

"Personally, I could never get over the shock," he says now, even though he still feels the fight against "subversives" was for a righteous cause. His first death flight so disturbed Scilingo that he went to a navy chaplain: "He told me that it was a Christian death because they did not suffer, that it was necessary to eliminate them."[69]

Walter Wink, in his article about reconciliation in Argentina, concludes:

> Belatedly, in 1995, senior bishops of the Roman Catholic Church in Argentina issued a statement expressing remorse for not having done more to prevent violence and government human rights abuses during the late 1970s. This lame facsimile of repentance did

---

[66] Emilio F. Mignone, *Witness to the Truth*, 8.
[67] Ibid., 10.
[68] Ibid., 10.
[69] Paul Gray, "*Waves from the Past*" in *Time* 47 (March 1995).

nothing to heal the loss of relatives of the disappeared. Mothers of the Plaza de Mayo, an Argentine human rights group, responded, "The Church knew that military chaplains participated at the jails in getting confessions from prisoners." The bishops did not "fail to do enough"; they actively supported a policy of State murder and human rights violations.[70]

d. Chile

In 1970, Salvador Allende Gossens become the first Marxist to be elected president by popular vote in Latin America. Between 1970 and 1973, president Salvadore Allende proposed radical changes: a democratic path to socialism. They met opposition from the right and the center political parties. In 1973, Chile was in turmoil. Inflation reached 500 percent. Shortages of food and consumer goods led to a series of violent strikes and demonstrations. On September 11, General Augusto Pinochet Ugarte, head of the army, took control of the country. The coup was supported by the right-wing parties and United States. President Allende died in the La Moneda presidential palace, and his ministers and collaborators were arrested and sent to concentration camps. Many of them were later killed or made to disappear.[71] The military junta in Chile was especially violent, with security forces responsible for the death or disappearance of 1,200 people by the end of the year. The Congress was dissolved, all political activity banned, and censorship was imposed. According to Amnesty International and the United Nations' Human Rights Committee, 250,000 Chileans had been detained for political reasons by the end of 1973. Summary executions, disappearances and killings in false armed confrontations became the norm. Neighbors, colleagues and others began denouncing each other, a practice encouraged by the military junta that became part of Chilean society at the beginning of the dictatorship.[72]

Thus began 17 years of military junta, which ended March 11, 1990. Within a few hours, the social conflict, which had permeated Chilean society immediately before the coup, was defined as a "war" and the concept of the "enemy within" as well as the National Security Doctrine were imposed throughout the nation. The enemy within was the Communist, the Marxist, the Socialist, the revolutionary, the subversive, indeed, anyone perceived by the military to constitute a challenge to the

---

[70] Walter Wink, *When the Powers Fall*, 46.
[71] Neil J. Kritz, *Transitional Justice*, Vol. 2, 453.
[72] Ibid., 453.

new established order.

The trend towards the restoration of democratic government, which swept through Latin America in the 1980's increased pressure for a limited political opening in Chile. Protests against Pinochet's rule and policies grew in the 1980s. In response, Pinochet declared a state of siege in August 1983. Eighteen thousand troops took to the streets and promptly arrested 1,200 people. In 1986, a demonstration and subsequent assassination attempt on Pinochet brought a new declaration of a state of siege and the arrest of 15,000 people. The ongoing and large-scale abuse of human rights drew international condemnation and isolation of Chile.[73] This meant that all legal cases involving infractions of State of Siege regulations were transferred from the civilian courts to war-time military institutions. These military concepts were used to justify the repression and killing unleashed upon Chile's population. The repression was not limited to one part of Chile, nor was it limited by social class, gender, profession, civil status or age.

The experience in Chile was similar in some ways to that of Argentina, but the Church in Chile took the lead in human rights defense. At first the hierarchy was publicly supportive of civilian rule to the end, but many bishops actually welcomed the coup when it came in September 1973. Most believed that the polarization of the Allende years had been harmful to the Church, that things could not have gone on as they had for most of 1972 and 1973, and that a coup was unavoidable. The bishops' first public statement as a group came on September 13, 1973. It was cautious and conciliatory, and gave tacit moral legitimacy to the new regime. It decried the spilling of "the blood of civilians and of soldiers," expressed trust in the "patriotism and selflessness" of the military, and asked citizens to cooperate so that institutional normalcy could be restored.[74] In the ensuing months, six of the thirty active bishops expressed their individual support for the coup. Some believed that conveying their concerns directly and personally to local military commanders would be more productive than "confronting" them. In some instances they were able to get clemency for specific individuals.[75] Nevertheless, early estimates were that as many as 1,200 were killed or disappeared in the first three months after the coup.[76]

Repression became more systematic and spread to small cities and rural areas in early 1974. The bishops' first criticism of regime abuse came in April, in their letter "Reconciliation in Chile!" They lamented the "climate of insecurity and fear" in the

[73] Neil J. Kritz, *Transitional Justice*, Vol. 2, 453.

[74] Jose Aldunate, "The Christian Ministry of Reconciliation in Chile" in Gregory Baum and Harold Wells, *The Reconciliation of Peoples: a Challenge to the Church*, 60-62.

[75] Brain H. Smith, *The Church and Politics in Chile* (Princeton, New Jersey: Princeton University Press, 1982), 288.

[76] Neil J. Kritz, *Transitional Justice*, Vol. 2, 453.

country and expressed concern over "interrogations, which include physical or moral constraints" but they hastened to affirm their confidence in the "good intentions" and "good will of our governmental authorities."[77]

Cardinal Silva of Santiago was a thorn in the military's side from the beginning. He was one of the first voices to call publicly for the early restoration of political freedoms and normal judicial processes. He also strongly opposed the military's "takeover" of the Catholic University of Santiago, of which he was the titular head. His opposition was based on his outrage at the government's extrajudicial persecution of its enemies. Military authorities took an immediate dislike to the cardinal. He led the resistance against the junta during its entire existence.[78]

In late September 1973, the Catholic, mainline Protestant, and Jewish communities had formed the National Committee to Aid Refugees (CONAR) to assist leftist émigrés who had come to Chile during the Allende years. In early October, Jewish and Lutheran leaders joined Cardinal Silva in forming the Cooperative Committee for Peace in Chile (COPACHI), whose mission was to provide legal and other assistance to people dismissed from their jobs, to those who had been detained or had "disappeared," and to their families. COPACHI programs provided people with safe havens in which they could share concerns, compare ideas and experiences, and coordinate future activities. Drawing on information from its provincial offices and from local churches, the organization prepared reports for the Church on arrests and disappearances, verified cases of torture, and was able to counter the lies and distortions of the controlled media.

The Church paid for its efforts in these regards. Harassment and arrest of COPACHI personnel (especially in Santiago), police raids on its service projects, and the detention of volunteers working in them, were all routine by early 1975. In addition, a quarter of the foreign priests (over 300 of the more than 1,200 in the country) were obliged to leave during the first two years of military rule.[79]

Even after two years of sustained violation of the civil, political, social, and economic rights of its citizens, the military received the public thanks of some bishops as a whole for having saved the country from Marxism. Yet, in September 1975, the hierarchy chose not to condemn them specifically, nor to raise fundamental questions about the structure of the political economy, which clearly violated the social teachings of the Church.[80]

---

[77] Michael Fleet and Brain H. Smith, *The Catholic Church and Democracy in Chile and Peru* (Notre Dame, Indiana: University of Notre Dame Press, 1997), 60.
[78] Ibid., 59-69.
[79] Michael Fleet and Brain H. Smith, *The Catholic Church and Democracy in Chile and Peru*, 62.
[80] Brain H. Smith, *The Church and Politics in Chile*, 296.

Later the Committee for Peace in Chile (COPACHI) was followed by the Vicariate of solidarity. The Vicariate was the rallying point of the resistance in Chile, and it did what it could to document torture and disappearance. Later, after 1990, the arrival of democracy permitted better opportunities to get to the truth about what had happened. The archives of the Vicariate of Solidarity helped the Commission for Truth and Reconciliation, the so-called Rettig Commission, to draw up a report. This report gives an account of the graver crimes committed by the military regime. It was done with such care and prudence that it elicited the consent of many who were in favor of the Armed Forces and the coup. It even elicited the respect of the injured parties who were seeking not only the truth but also justice. The Rettig Report has certainly been an important step on the long road to reconciliation.[81]

One major reason for this deference was that some bishops still believed it possible to influence government leaders through private negotiations. A good number continued to maintain good personal relations with representatives of the government in their provinces, and were treated respectfully and cordially by local military commanders. Hence, many bishops still did not take a systemic view of the deeper structural contradictions that were causing both economic exploitation and political repression, and believed that quiet diplomacy was the best strategy for them to employ in order to alleviate the abuses that did exist.

The second reason was the Chilean Church was quite vulnerable in its dealings with State authorities. Its schools were dependent on public subsidies, and half of its priests were foreigners serving in Chile at the good graces of the military government. Pinochet's government exploited these dependencies and periodically intimidated Catholic bishops in an effort, often successful, to limit the scope of their activities.[82] Finally on March 25, 1977, after three and a half years the Catholic Bishops Conferees of Chile called for an end to government by decree implying that the military were not the legitimate representatives of the people, and urged popular ratification of any future constitution or set of law:

> We believe that there will not exist full guarantees for the respect of human rights so long as the country does not have a constitution, old or new, ratified by popular vote. Such guarantees will also be lacking so long as laws are not written by legitimate representatives of the citizenry, or while all the structures of the state, from the highest to the lowest, are not subject to the constitution and to a set of laws. [83]

---

[81] Gregory Baum and Harold Wells, *The Reconciliation of Peoples: a Challenge to the Church*, 62- 63.

[82] Michael Fleet and Brain H. Smith, *The Catholic Church and Democracy in Chile and Peru*, 74.

[83] Brain H. Smith, *The Church and Politics in Chile*, 309.

Relations with the regime and the Church never did improve. Since the 1980's bishops do not limit themselves to making a call to the conscience; they also seek structural and institutional changes. In December 1980 a group of seven bishops issued a decree of excommunication for those responsible for torture, not only those participating in the actual torture but also those who ordered it or were in a position to stop it but did not. In December of 1983 the entire Bishops' Conference subscribed to the excommunication for torturers and their accomplices.[84] In January 1987, prompted in part by the forthcoming visit to Chile of Pope John Paul II, the state of siege was lifted. Two months later, non-Marxist political parties were permitted to register. Notwithstanding these positive developments, the security forces maintained a significant degree of political repression. In 1988, confident that Chilean society would not oppose him, Pinochet consented to a plebiscite allowing the population to vote for or against his continued rule. A peaceful political campaign resulted in a "No" victory, paving the way for general elections in 1989. Christian Democrat Patricio Aylwin won the presidency and assumed office in March 1990. General Pinochet remained Commander-in-Chief of the Army through 1997.[85]

Following the example of the new democracy in Argentina, the president appointed a National Commission on Truth and Reconciliation. Its findings were made public but a rash of assassinations led to the effective suppression of the report.[86] The investigation attempted to establish the number of detainees who were "disappeared," and did not include those who were simply tortured. Nor did it name the perpetrators. The new civil government in Chile created a "Commission of Reparation and Reconciliation" to complement the work of the earlier commission by providing a modest but decent pension for families of the disappeared, as well as scholarships, health care, and military exemptions. Returned exiles and those expelled from employment were paid reparation. Conflicts over the legacy of the Pinochet regime continued to confront society. After the end of junta churches were playing a central role in the demanding for truth-telling and reconciliation.[87]

Jose Aldunate in his article "The Christian Ministry of Reconciliation in Chile" writes:

> Despite some successful advances in which the Church has played a part, Christians must face the fact that in Chile the important

---

[84] Ibid., 311.
[85] Neil J. Kritz, *Transitional Justice*, Vol. 2 (1995): 454.
[86] Ibid., 454.
[87] Walter Wink, *When the Powers Fall*, 47-48.

task of reconciliation still remains largely unfulfilled. The reconciliation between rich and poor has been left unresolved. It will not be attained through fiche preaching but only through basic economic changes infused with a spirit of justice. Also unfulfilled is the reconciliation of political activists. This does not demand a common program, but it calls for a *metanoia* through adherence to democracy and service to the common good. Reconciliation needs to move forward among groups of people who are still imbued with ideologies. They must learn to acknowledge the human dignity, of those they, have injured, make restitution, offer forgiveness and accept that no one is deserving of hate or ought to be excluded from fraternal coexistence.

We would like to see our churches, which on occasion have motivated fanaticism and violence, turn to these challenges by going beyond the restricted world of parishes and sacraments. They have been called by Vatican Council II to defend and promote human dignity in a new world that is entailing the third millennium.[88]

In Conclusion

In Argentina and Chile, there were similar political situations. But the Church's approach to the situations was so different. In Chile the Church was seeking truth and reconciliation. However, in Argentina the Church was involved in collaboration with the military junta. What is it that made such a difference in these two countries? Because of the Church's hierarchical structure, the leading hierarchy played a significant role. In Argentina, preeminent bishops supported the regime. In Chile, Cardinal Silva opposed the regime. In Argentina, the Church always identified herself with rich and conservative circles, whereas in Chile the Church had experience and tradition in dealing with social issues even before the junta.

Different cultures deal with reconciliation differently. First, it depends on what resources the Church has to deal with reconciliation. How powers shifted when oppression ended made a difference in how the culture dealt with reconciliation. What resources did the Church have in dealing with reconciliation? The Church in most cases during oppression remains an active independent voice from the regime. In those incidents the Church plays a central role in resisting the oppressors. Often the oppressors try to divide the Church. If they succeed as it happened in France and Argentina, it is difficult for the Church to assist in the process of reconciliation. In

---

[88] Jose Aldunate, "The Christian Ministry of Reconciliation in Chile," 63.

these incidents, the Church has to go through the process of repentance as an institution.

In the new democratic regimes, justice comes quickly or it does not come at all. In France within two years it was done. Later, the idea of a purge in the Church was not acceptable to society. The same situation existed in Chile and Argentina. After a few years the army gave self-amnesty. Another difficulty for the Church dealing with reconciliation is that in many countries, churches cling to traditional authoritarianism, and are a hindrance rather than a help to democratization.[89] Studies of the process of reconciliation in various countries are helpful in looking at how the Lithuanian Catholic Church dealt with reconciliation after the fall of communism.

---

[89] Walter Wink, *When the Powers Fall*, 63.

CHAPTER FOUR:
RENEWED PRACTICE

A. Introduction

More than ten years have passed since the collapse of the Soviet regime in Lithuania. Church and State can operate freely. At first glance, there seems to be no reason to discuss reconciliation because oppression was long ago and everyone is free. But this is just the first impression. If we do a deep analysis of society and the Church, we realize that we need to discuss this topic. From my conversations with former dissidents, I have observed social changes in a society where the rich are becoming richer and the poor even poorer. Looking at our political situation there is a big division between right and left wing political parties. It is becoming clear that we need to talk about reconciliation in our society and especially social reconciliation. We have to talk about reconciliation within Roman Catholic circles as well.

One Lithuanian bishop visited our parish in Chicago. I asked him, "What are the former collaborators doing in the Lithuanian Roman Catholic Church now?" I did not expect such a straightforward answer from the bishop: "They are in charge of almost everything even after ten years of independence." It seems that the question concerning reconciliation within the Catholic Church is important these days. What happened during the first years of independence was very important because it gave direction to the process of reconciliation.

B. The State and Reconciliation

In the late 1980's, as a period of reform and liberalization unfolded under Soviet leader Mikhail Gorbachev, a renewed sense of nationalism gained strength in Lithuania, displayed in public demonstrations and in the mass media. In 1988, the formation of independent political groups was permitted. Most prominent among them was the Lithuanian Movement for Support of *Perestroika*, *Sąjūdis*, which called for autonomy from the Soviet Union. Vytautas Landsbergis was elected its president.

On May 19, 1989, the parliament (Supreme Council) declared Lithuanian sovereignty and the supremacy of Lithuanian law over Soviet law. In February 1990, *Sajūdis* candidates won the elections to the Parliament of Lithuania by an overwhelming majority. Shortly thereafter, Landsbergis was elected chairman of the Supreme Council and Kazimiera Prunskienė of *Sajūdis* was elected prime minister.[1]

On March 11, 1990, Lithuania declared its independence. The difficult transition period leading up to independence *de facto* and *de jure* commenced. The Soviets responded by seizing Communist Party buildings in Vilnius and cutting off shipments of oil, gas, and other raw materials. The talks between Moscow and Vilnius made little progress. In January 11-13, 1991, Soviet troops seized the Lithuanian Television, radio and other vital state institutions. Fourteen Lithuanians were killed at the Vilnius Television tower; hundreds were injured. Tensions continued to mount between Moscow and Vilnius.[2]

Following the failed August 1991 coup attempt in Moscow, Soviet power structures began to falter. Much of the international community granted diplomatic recognition to independent Lithuania, Latvia, and Estonia. Finally, on September 6, 1991, the Soviet Union formally recognized the independence of Lithuania.[3]

After independence, one of the most delicate issues involving reconciliation was what the State should do with former wrongdoers, collaborators with the Soviet regime. Concern over previous collaboration by Lithuanian officials with the Soviet secret police became a highly charged political issue. On November 12, 1991, the government decreed that former KGB employees and informers could not hold local or national government posts for five years. Those already holding such positions were required to resign by the end of the year. A December 1991 law created a parliamentary commission (known as the Gajauskas Commission for its chairman) to investigate collaboration with the KGB by elected representatives. Among those accused by the Commission were former Prime Minister Prunskienė and Deputy of Parliament Virgilijus Čepaitis, a close associate of Landsbergis and an advocate of decommunization.[4]

Before the October 1992 parliamentary elections, all candidates were required to declare whether they had ever been connected with the KGB, other State security services, or the Communist Party. Screening of collaborators was complicated by the KGB's earlier removal of much of its Lithuanian files to Russia. Following extensive negotiations with Russia, some of the files were returned in 1992. In November 1992,

---

[1] Alfred Erich Senn, *Lithuanian Awakening* (Los Angeles: University of California Press, 1990), 255-260.
[2] Neil J. Kritz, *Transitional Justice*, Washington, D.C.: United States Institute of Peace Press, Vol. 2, 763.
[3] Ibid., 764.
[4] Neil J. Kritz, *Transitional Justice,* 764.

parliament declared the KGB files to be part of the Lithuanian "national heritage," barring their destruction or removal from the country. In 1993, partly on the basis of these records, the government issued warrants for the arrest of several individuals allegedly responsible for the January 1991 Vilnius crackdown.[5]

A 1991 decree ordered that property of the Lithuanian Communist Party and affiliated organizations be confiscated. A 1991 law on property restitution enabled former owners or their heirs to petition to reclaim property nationalized during Communist rule. Based on the nature of the property involved, claimants would receive the actual property, a property of equivalent value, or financial compensation.[6] People who had been deported to Siberia or sent into exile elsewhere in the former Soviet Union and political prisoners received the privilege of public transportation discounts and increased pensions, but when economic conditions worsened in 1997, some of these privileges were lost.

Late with these efforts, the political pendulum swung away from full-scale decommunization. Having achieved their common goal of Lithuanian independence, the various factions within *Sajūdis* began to splinter. A deteriorating economy under the *Sajūdis*-led government also reduced public confidence in the party. As a result, the Lithuanian Democratic Labor Party (LDLP), successor to the now-banned Communist Party, won the parliamentary election of October 25, 1992 by a large margin. LDLP leader Algirdas Brazauskas was elected chairman of the Supreme Council, replacing Landsbergis. On February 14, 1993, Brazauskas was elected president of Lithuania. From that time former Communist functionaries continued to dominate in Lithuanian government and Lithuanian's economic life: they continued economic reform, but they stopped the truth telling process and ignored the question of justice.[7]

It was difficult for the new State to seek reconciliation. One of the reasons for the difficulty was that the former communist elite remained strong and had always had political and economical influence. When independence came, Lithuania did not have its own government and lacked experienced people to lead the country.

The United States Institute of Peace printed a three-volume study about the truth telling problem in thirty newly liberated countries in Africa, Latin America and Europe. From those case studies the Institute of Peace suggested a number of rules:

1. The truth needs to be told, and it needs to be told completely.

2. If the threat posed by the old regime and its forces prevents full disclosure, then as much should be revealed as is possible.

---

[5] Ibid., 764-65.
[6] Neil J. Kritz, *Transitional Justice*, 763-765.
[7] Ibid., 795.

3. The truth needs to be sanctioned by an official body. If the new government is too weak to do it, then it should be done by the churches.

4. At least the leading architects and executors of the policy of disappearances, murder, and torture should be prosecuted. If they cannot be prosecuted, they should at least be publicly exposed.

5. Amnesty should not be offered until the truth has been told and, if possible, at least some of those most guilty prosecuted.[8]

Walter Wink, in his book *When the Powers Fall*, writes, " Society recovering from the trauma of State violence needs as much truth as possible. Truth is medicine. Without it, a society remains infected with past evils that will inevitably break out in the future… Truth telling not only exposes that lie, but establishes a sacred space where others may gather who no longer tolerate the lie, as in the churches of East Germany. It is the responsibility of religious communities to see that the truth gets told and to provide that space. Those cases where they have done so are a light in our darkness."[9]

C. The Lithuanian Church and Reconciliation

From my fieldwork, interviews with former dissidents and KGB archives, it is clear that a small group of the clergy, religious and lay people in the Church heroically resisted the Soviet regime while the greater number remained silent. Maybe the latter did not have enough strength or opportunity or health to resist the oppressor. Some of them led a silent resistance. But there was a small group of Church people who profited from the occupation regime. For their silence they had better positions, privileges to travel, etc. It was a very small group, though, that collaborated with the Soviets voluntarily.

During the first years of independence, the Church had a great deal of authority within society. The reason for this was that the Church was the only institution that was able during the Soviet regime to organize systematic resistance against the oppressors. But the Church had collaborators within its circles. What was the position the Church took with former collaborators? The best answer to this question would probably be the following two paragraphs from Robert J. Schreiter's book *Reconciliation, Mission and Ministry in a Changing Social Order* where he characterizes how the Church as an institution reacts when the oppressing regime is

---

[8] Neil J. Kritz, *Transitional Justice,*
[9] Walter Wink, *When the Powers Fall* (Minneapolis: Fortress Press, 1998), 53-54.

gone. Lithuania is an ideal example of this.

> Churches, for all their wrapping themselves in the mantle of the prophet, usually end up reflecting the tensions and divisions of the larger society, especially when the churches themselves are quite large and are coextensive with large segments of the population. To some extent, this comes as no surprise. Church leaders, who are concerned about preserving the unity of the Church, are keenly aware of how damaging divisiveness is to the Church as the body of Christ. While that concern for patient attention to all and to inclusion is important, it cannot be used as an excuse for trucking with the narrative of the lie. The Church must stand for truth in its entirety and with all its discomfort if it is to witness to the gospel of Jesus Christ.
>
> Likewise, the Church cannot assume automatically that it has a mediating role between victims and oppressors. Because the Church mirrors society, it may find that the lines dividing society run right through the center of the Church. We noted this (in the first chapter), pointing out that some members of the Church choose to collaborate with an oppressive regime in order to allow for some public activity on the part of the Church. Others choose the path of resistance and utter opposition to the regime, paying for their stance with imprisonment, exile, and even death. Sometimes Church leaders side with an oppressive government for the sake of "peace," while some of their local clergy and members choose opposition. The ministry of reconciliation is not just something that the Church exercises; at times the Church is in need of that ministry itself. Reconciliation within the Church can be as necessary as reconciliation within the larger society.[10]

These two paragraphs really tell what has happened, more specifically what has not happened, in the Lithuanian Catholic Church after oppression ended. Did the Church even try to achieve reconciliation within Church circles? The Church as an institution failed to do that. Of course, at the very beginning there were some attempts. One of the high officials of the seminary was removed. But after a few years, the man who replaced him was removed as well because the Church hierarchy succumbed to the pressure of the former clergy who had collaborated. When two

---

[10] Robert Schreiter, *Reconciliation: Mission and Ministry in a Changing Social Order* (Maryknoll, NY: Orbis Books, 1999), 67.

bishops who had lived in exile returned to their metropolitan sees, one or two people from the chancery offices were removed.

During the first years of *Perestroika*, but before Lithuania's independence, one priest who was a notorious collaborator died in a car accident. He was driving to change his money. At that time the Lithuanian government moved from Soviet rubles to a national currency. He had a great deal of Soviet rubles because during the Soviet regime the printing of holy cards was prohibited, but he had permission from the Soviets to print these cards, to sell religious vestments, print catechisms. This was tolerated by the Soviet regime. Others who tried to publish religious materials were punished. Usually, priests are buried in the churchyard. In this case, for what he had done during the Soviet period, the archbishop did not allow him to be buried in the churchyard. This caused a great deal of controversy and even caused a fight during the funeral. These events caused great tension within Church circles.

It is as Robert Schreiter says, "Because the Church mirrors society, it may find that the lines dividing society run right through the center of the Church..."[11] Soon the Church leadership found that the removal of former collaborators was a difficult issue. Even right after independence, two noted dissident bishops who had been in exile were given two metropolitan sees. Another former dissident was named a bishop. But even in these situations the Church remained silent and never spoke about wrongdoers in Church circles.

The situation after *Perestroika* in the Lithuanian Catholic Church, though not identical, was very close to the experience of the Russian Orthodox Church. During the Soviet regime all the hierarchy in Russia was forced to collaborate. Both the Soviet government and the Russian Orthodox Church hierarchy persecuted dissidents in the Russian Orthodox Church. In the situation after *Perestroika* the Russian Orthodox Church had no strength or resources to deal with the process of reconciliation. The Russian Orthodox Church is in fact the only national Soviet-style institution still surviving in Russia today, in that its leadership remains largely unchanged from Soviet times.[12] For example, Patriarch Alexei II was accused of being a long-term KGB agent, but no major inquiry or public debate has followed.[13] The same situation occurred in Lithuania when the book *Akiplėša*[14] was printed, or an

---

[11] Robert Schreiter, *Reconciliation: Mission and Ministry in a Changing Social Order*, 67.

[12] Philip Walters,"The Russian Orthodox Church and Foreign Christianity the Legacy of the Past" in John Witte Jr. and Michael Bordeaux (ed), *Proselytism and Orthodoxy in Russia* (Maryknoll, New York: Orbis Books, 1999), 183.

[13] Joan Lofgren, " Reconciliation in the Soviet Past" in Liucia Ann McSpadden (ed), *Reaching Reconciliation* (Uppsala, Sweden: Life & Peace Institute, 2000), 177.

[14] Spengla V. "Akiplėša," KGB file on Rev. Juozas Zdebskis. Vilnius.1996 Akiplėša (Eng. "Impudent One") was the KGB's codename for a priest they persecuted, Juozas Zdebskis. From this file it is clear

article in *Naujasis Židinys*[15] disclosing that some of the priests and bishops had collaborated. There was no reaction in either Church circles or in society.

Until today, there have been no changes in some of the dioceses of Lithuania from Soviet times. Of course, the Lithuanian situation is a little different from the Russian situation because during the Soviet regime the Lithuanian Church administrators were not brave enough to silence those who resisted. They would have lost their authority with the people. But when the Church did not deal with reconciliation within itself, this brought the Church to a similar situation as was found in the Russian Orthodox Church. And the situation in Lithuania was not so "easy" as in Poland or Germany, where only a few clergy had collaborated with the secret service or *Stasi*. Removing them was easy.[16]

In those cases where the truth was told, Walter Wink says that there was light in the darkness.[17] Unfortunately, the official position of the Lithuanian Church was to stay in the darkness. Truth telling does not happen. The Church neither told the truth about those who collaborated nor were they removed from positions of authority. One of the more famous dissidents, who at that time was a bishop, wrote in *The Chronicle* in 1991:

> Those who were carrying out the genocide of the Nation and for the Church realized that in order for deceit and oppression to succeed, dark secrecy is required. Only in the dark can works of darkness be carried out. On the other hand, those who were concerned about the future of Lithuania and the Church likewise understood that the only way to fight successfully against the wiles of deceit and oppression is to expose their evil to light.[18]

During the Soviet regime, dissidents understood how important telling the truth was. In the first days of independence the Church leaders "forgot" how important truth telling was. They thought that in this way they were preserving the

---

that the Soviets murdered him by setting up a car accident. Some priest collaborators even provided informaiton necessary for setting up the accident.

[15] Arūnas Streikus, "Ganytojiško darbo atnaujinimas ir tęstinumas" in *Naujasia Židinys* , Magazine, 2002, No. 1/2 .

[16] Mary L. Gautier, "Church Elites and the Restoration of Civil Society in the Communist Societies of Central Europe" in Derek H. Davis (ed), *Journal of Church and State,* No. 2 Philadelphia, Spring 1998, 289-371.

[17] Walter Wink, *When the Powers Fall,* 54.

[18] *Lietuvos Katalikų Bažnyčios Kronika* (Chronicle of the Catholic Church in Lithuania), Chicago: The Society of the Chronicle of Lithuania, Vol. 10, xiii.

unity of the Church. The truth was not told. This has had a long lasting consequence for the Church and for society. Lithuanian Catholic Church leaders, in regard to truth telling, took the position of "forgive and forget." Is that in the Bible? No. The Caritas International Handbook *Working for Reconciliation*, notes:

> The injunction "forgive and forget" is found nowhere in the Bible. It appears to have come from medieval Western Christianity. The issue is that we can never forget profound evil that has been perpetrated upon us. To forget either trivializes the evil or trivializes our dignity as human beings. It would be better to say that in forgiving we never forget, but we do learn to remember in a different way. That is to say, the way we remember what has happened no longer detracts from our humanity, but has become part of a reconciliation process that has restored our humanity. It also gives us a new perspective on the wrongdoer who has perpetrated the evil against us: as someone also bereft of humanity as a result of that deed. A stark example of this is found in John's Gospel. When Jesus appeared to his disciples after the resurrection, his transfigured body - that could walk through locked doors - still bore the scars of his torture. But those wounds are no longer lingering recriminations of those who had tortured him. They had become sources for healing the lack of faith of the disciples and the doubts of Thomas. What has happened to us can never be erased. But it can be seen in a different way, which empowers the victim rather than being a continuing source of degradation.[19]

From my interviews with former dissidents, especially with those for whom reconciliation is a very difficult issue, I learned that these dissidents feel that not telling the truth about what happened victimizes them again. This is one of the obstacles to their moving toward reconciliation.

The return of freedom and independence created a disturbance in the Catholic Church of Lithuania. The Church was very popular during the first year of independence. It was in vogue to donate money to the Church and to adhere to the advice of a Church representative. Churches were overcrowded during that first year. Priests were invited everywhere: to every meeting and demonstration, to appear on television, to bless every establishment, store, bank and even businesses newly

---

[19] Brian Starken (ed), *Working for Reconciliation A Caritas Handbook* (Vatican City: Caritas Internationalis, 1999), 40.

founded by former functionaries of the communist era. Many of these blessed banks lured investments from trusting customers by offering high interest rates on savings. However, since they operated on a pyramid principle they went bankrupt in a few years' time, with millions of their customers' hard earned money having disappeared. What was it those post-soviet bankers needed? Was it the blessing itself or the cover of the then very popular Church?

The initial euphoria wore off quickly and the everyday set in. It seemed that with society's climate having changed, the view of the Church also changed. Then the search for enemies continued, and that which is searched for surely is found. Those who thought a little differently than the majority of the conservative Church were labeled either enemies of the Church, enemies of independence or as communists. During the first decade of independence the dominant viewpoint of the Catholic Church of Lithuania was that all that is the Church is good (including even those priests and the religious who had been KGB agents and had collaborated with the Soviet regime) and the world outside the Church is evil. And one does not tolerate evil; one fights it! While the battles with windmills were being waged, other religious denominations began to move in and challenge the sole authority of the Catholic Church.

The Catholic Church was the only organization in the Soviet Union that was controlled from abroad. For that reason a great amount of attention was paid to the seminary, since the future of the Church depended upon the quality of the preparation of the priests. The Soviet government tried to infiltrate the ranks of the seminary professors and students with its recruited agents. Through all its years of existence, *The Chronicle* relentlessly criticized seminary activity in almost every issue, reminding readers of government interference, KGB-recruited seminarians, and instructors who were government collaborators. *The Chronicle* even radically posited that more than ninety percent of the seminary population consisted of recruited soviet agents.[20]

Finally the Church could act freely, hire instructors, and rid the seminary of collaborators. Former dissidents, supported by the Vatican and society at large, had the most influence in its hierarchical structure. And lo, what a miracle has taken place: all of the collaborators have "disappeared." Though over many years practically no changes have occurred in the leadership of the seminary, the collaborating instructors of whom *The Chronicle* wrote with such zealousness had "disappeared." The "psychologically ill," soviet-recruited clerics *The Chronicle* told of had "disappeared"

---

[20] Saulius Suziedelis, *The Sword and the Cross* (Huntington, Indiana: Our Sunday Visitor Publishing Division, 1988), 225.

as well. Nothing changed in the seminary; no one was fired or punished. What did happen was that the most fundamental principal of both a democratic society and of reconciliation was forgotten.

The Church now adopted rules that had been outlined by the KGB and other institutions of the former repressive government. After independence was regained, all the members of the Church hierarchy who had collaborated with the Soviet government "disappeared" as well. True, one of them was transferred from a metropolitan archdiocese to an "insignificant" diocese, where for an entire decade he managed that diocese as if the dark era of soviet persecution had not yet passed.

Were there any consequences to the lack of truth telling in the Catholic Church? The following is one such instance: In 1978, *The Chronicle* printed an article listing the priests who were fostering a KGB agent. This same article states: "A year IV cleric, Ričardas Jakutis, suspected for some time of being a KGB agent, was expelled from the Kaunas Priests Seminary for drinking and womanizing." *The Chronicle* article further comments on the behavior of Church administrators: "During a meeting in 1978, the head of the Archdiocese of Vilnius, E. Krivaitis, demanded that Jakutis be returned to the seminary on the grounds that he had been slandered without foundation (after a public admission)." Notwithstanding the evidence, which a few witnesses provided, Jakutis was returned to the seminary and later ordained a priest. Still, the publishers of *The Chronicle* raise a question at the end of the article: "When will this story end? When will a public sinner and KGB agent finally be run out of the seminary?"[21]

With the disappearance of the Soviet regime, the Church hierarchy adopted the medieval Christian principle "forgive and forget." It seems as though Father Jakutis, as well as other collaborators, "disappeared." But lo and behold, he unexpectedly "reappeared." His name was splashed across the largest daily newspapers in the country. One of them, *Lietuvos Aidas*, wrote: "The court has determined that from April 1994 through the beginning of 1997, R. Jakutis borrowed large sums of money from banks, various establishments and private citizens, never intending to repay them. He covered up his criminal activity with a fictitious non-profit organization called Family of Hope. With talk of future construction of orphanages, homes for the elderly and for the disabled, the former priest lured money from his creditors. In fact, his organization did not concern itself with construction of any kind, or with any bookkeeping, and no project ever reached fruition. Twenty-eight plaintiffs were

---

[21] *Lietuvos Katalikų Bažnyčios Kronika* (Chronicle of the Catholic Church in Lithuania), Chicago: The Society of the Chronicle of Lithuania, Vol. 5, 93-94.

seeking to reclaim approximately 11 million *litas* (just over 2.5 million dollars)."[22]

In 1999, Father Algis Gudaitis, SJ shared his comments on the situation with foreign journalists: "I'd say some priests and even some bishops are too active in politics. This isn't appropriate. Priests sometimes side with parties to make their lives more comfortable. Some have even benefited financially. I think we'll find that priests who took money and maintained links to the previous government are the same ones who collaborated with the KGB. They feared being exposed and tried to support the left wing when the left was recently in power. Maybe they will be exposed now that the Conservatives are at the helm."[23] Unfortunately, though political parties changed, the Church's policy to "forget" did not change, and the scandals that often plague the Church very clearly illustrate the extremely negative effects of the lack of truthfulness.

After the end of the Soviet era the term *homo sovieticus* was developed and often used. It was used even in the Lithuanian Catholic Church to describe what the Soviet regime did to our dignity and humanity. We can define *homo sovieticus* in the following way: The base of socialism was an unwritten contract; the citizen was not to attempt to interfere in public life, and the State would guarantee a problem-free vegetation (neither poor nor rich). To this end, the State would tolerate almost everything: a poor work ethic, petty theft of communal property, irresponsible and inconsiderate behavior toward nature and neighbor. This contract logically led to moral corruption and disintegration of values on a scale previously unknown. Marxism did in fact cultivate a new man, but one about as far from the "superman" of socialist realism novels as Sancho Panza was from Don Quixote. The *homo sovieticus* was the ultimate conformer, lacking all creativity, responsibility, and initiative. The Soviet Man may have been the ideal contractual partner for the Soviet State. Though he gave up his claim to conscience, he was taught to forget both his history and his past.

The noted writer Chingiz Aitmatov in the 1980's wrote a book *The Day Lasts More than a Hundred Years*. At that time this was almost as famous as Aleksandr Solzhenitsyn's book *One Day in the Life of Ivan Denisovich*. Aitmatov tells us one legend concerning a tribe of people in a central Asian territory of the Soviet Union:

> The Zhuan'zhuan tribe treated captive warriors with exceptional cruelty. Those who were sold into slavery in neighboring lands were

---

[22] Ričardas Jakutis, "Nuteistas pusseptintų metų kalėti" in *Lietuvos Aidas*, No. 95 (18 May 1999), (7842).
[23] Howard Jarvis, "An Interview with Father Algis Gudaitis" in *The Baltics Worldwide*, Magazine, No. 7 Vilnius, 1999.

considered fortunate, because sooner or later they could escape and return to their homeland. But a monstrous fate awaited those whom the Zhuan'zhuan kept as slaves for themselves. They destroyed their slaves' memory by a terrible torture - the putting of the *shiri* onto the head of the victim. This fate was reserved for young men captured in battle. First of all their heads were completely shaved and every single hair was taken out by the root. When this was completed, expert Zhuan'zhuan butchers killed a nearby nursing mother camel and skinned it. First they removed the heavy udder with its matted hair. Then they divided it into several pieces and, in its still warm state, stretched it over the shaven heads of the prisoners. At once it stuck in place like a sticking plaster, looking rather like a present-day swimming cap. [*In the heat of the desert sun the camel-skin plaster shrank as it dried causing unbearable pressure on the man's skull – author's note.*] The man who was subjected to the ensuing torture either died because he could not stand it, or he lost his memory of the past forever. He had become a *mankurt*, or slave, who could not remember his past life.[24]

Later in this legend he tells about one *mankurt* whose mother finds him, but because he was not able to remember his past and his mother, Zhuan'zhuan tribe members forced him to kill his mother. This legend was used to describe the mentality of *homo sovieticus*, about the danger of forgetting and the importance of truth telling. During *Perestroika* many priests preached about *homo sovieticus* and the legend about *mankurt*, but they always applied it to society and not to the Church. But indeed, truth telling is important for society and for the Church as well. Post-communist societies were divided between those who collaborated and those who did not. One sad thing in the Lithuanian Church now is that the KGB had drawn the line of division during the Soviet regime, and throughout *Perestroika* no one told the truth in order to redraw this line.

Leaders of the Roman Catholic Church in Lithuania were not prepared to accept this new spirit in the world and remained in semi-isolation. The strong mentality of Christendom and the theology of resistance, which was formed during the Russian Empire and Soviet period, did not help in the renewal of the Catholic Church or in the process of reconciliation. During the reigns of the czars and Soviet occupations Lithuanian nationalism had long been associated with the Catholic faith, and it was the loyalty of Lithuanians to the faith of their fathers against Orthodox

---

[24] Chingiz Aitmatov, *The Day Lasts More than a Hundred Years* (Bloomington, Indiana: University Press, 1988), 124-25.

Russia. The result was that loyalty to the Catholic faith in Lithuania was a political statement. But for this same reason, the Church in Lithuania has had a rather conservative appearance up to the present day. There is a long way to go.

Today pastoral care still concentrates upon the immortality of the soul as the chief interest of the Church. James F. White, in his book *Christian Worship*, writes: "Roman Catholic tradition remained the most firmly committed to late medieval ways of worship, especially since it was often forced into a defensive position."[25] The Church in Lithuania for centuries was in a defensive position and I can name many medieval forms of pastoral care. The preparation for first communion and confession are from a catechism that is one hundred years old. The first edition was printed in 1911. This catechism begins with an image of God as provident, giving immediate reward and punishment for good and evil deeds in this world. Vatican II made many changes in the Church, including a new image of God who is reconciling and who is loving. But in Lithuania the catechism of one hundred years ago is still used.[26]

One of the most vivid examples that the spirit of Christendom is alive is the construction of many new churches in Lithuania. Most of these churches are being built in the old, traditional, expensive way with three naves, two towers, and big churchyards. During Soviet times there was a need to demonstrate that the Church was large and powerful. This corresponds to the idea of Christendom, which is a strong powerful Church. Because these two institutions, the Church and the Soviet Union, were fighting, the Church needed a powerful institution. But now churches built in this way are causing problems. Some of the faithful cannot understand why such large churches are being built, at the expense of programs for evangelization and sacramental preparation, the training of lay people and helping the poor. Unfortunately, many leaders are working toward reestablishing the Catholic Church and Christendom as it was known prior to the Vatican II.

Church historian John C. Dwyer in his book, *Church History*, confirms this concept. "There was a problem in Hungary and in many other parts of Eastern Europe which a number of American Catholics never recognized: some of the very churchmen who were heroic defenders of the rights of the Church were committed to an outdated social and economical order, and were arch-conservative, not only in Church matters, but in political matters as well."[27] One of the difficulties in the Lithuanian Catholic Church in our day is those priests who were so active in the resistance. They know just two ways of acting: to be oppressed or to be oppressors. In many situations they are

---

[25] James F. White, *A Brief History of Christian Worship* (Nashville: Abigdon Press, 1993), 106.
[26] Compare Kazimieras Paltarokas, *Katalikų Tikybos Katekizmas* (Kaunas: Žemaičių vyskupija 1913) with Kazimieras Paltarokas, *Trumpas Katalikų Katekizmas* (Kaunas: XXI amžius, 1999).
[27] John C. Dwyer, *Church History* (New York: Paulist Press, 1985), 375.

acting as their former KGB persecutors acted.

Even though the Church was spoken of highly at the onset of independence, in more recent years there has been more and more talk of a Church in crisis. Only in 2000, a jubilee year, when Vatican directives required a Mass of Reconciliation to mark the occasion, did the Catholic Church for the first time officially acknowledge and issue an apology for its collaboration. A lay person who was a former political prisoner and champion of freedom of conscience, read the invocation of apology for collaboration: "We acknowledge that members of our Church, because of human weakness, fear, and sometimes for personal gain accommodated criminal occupying regimes and even acted on behalf of those who would crush freedom and justice. Let us pray that the wounds of these sins be healed."[28] It is a mystery why it was decided that a layman, a former prisoner of conscience, would read this invocation when those who collaborated and who did the most harm were among the most influential in the Church: priests or Church administrators. These words, while vague, were the first spoken on the subject in more than ten years since the Soviet occupying regime had gone.

How is the Church perceived now, ten years having passed from the reestablishment of Lithuania's independence? It is perceived as a relic of the past though it is still respected for its bearing during the Soviet era. However, during this period of regained independence, the Church is struggling to communicate with the new generation and a society in the throes of modernization. The illusion of Lithuania as a particularly Catholic country, called the Land of Mary, has dissipated. The Lithuania of today can more likely be described as poor, a country of pessimists and a disharmonious society; it has the highest suicide rate in Europe, is unable to curb crime, and has a high divorce rate.[29]

What role has the Church played during this ten-year period? It has played a very limited role because in order to influence society the Church must renew itself perpetually, address problems and issues from its first era. The Church must not live on its "sclerotic traditions,"[30] as Cardinal Suenen has said.

To talk about the crisis of faith within the organization of the hierarchy of the Lithuanian Catholic Church is not popular. But there are many who understand the situation. Eglė Laumenskaitė of the Center for Religious Studies at Vilnius University paints a gloomy picture. She says while some two thirds of the population claim to be

---

[28] Lietuvos Vyskupų Konferencijos 2000 metų Jubiliejaus komitetas, "Atgailos ir Atsiprašymo pamaldų intencijos ir maldos," April 14, 2000.
[29] See Jolanta Rimkutė and Edita Vološčiuk (ed), *Pranešimas apie žmogaus socialinę raidą Lietuvoje 2001* (Vilnius: Jungtinių Tautų vystymo programa, 2001).
[30] John C. Dwyer, *Church History*, 354.

Catholic, only about a fifth actually practice the faith regularly. Most go to church infrequently—mostly on the occasion of weddings, funerals or holidays. Laumenskaitė pins the blame on the Soviet era, which, she says, spoiled the sense of community among Lithuanians. "Christianity cannot exist without this sense of community," she said. "People are reluctant to come together. Trust has been lost and replaced by extreme individualism—a simple extension of Communist ideology, which itself stressed material well-being."[31]

Another problem is the Church itself. To its own detriment, says Laumenskaitė, it has not been able to reject the confrontational approach it put to such good use in Soviet days. Said Laumenskaitė: "Resistance to the Soviet system fostered a siege mentality which doesn't correspond to liberalization and the openness encouraged by Vatican II."[32] Ironically, the most Catholic nation among former Soviet republics is also one of the only nations anywhere in Europe that has seen something of a pagan revival. Lithuania was the last nation in Europe to be Christianized—1,000 years after France[33]—and this late turn to the Christian God has always been evident in the way even the Church so readily mixes Christian with pre-Christian symbols. Nevertheless, the actual resurgence of Lithuania's old pantheistic religion has alarmed some Church leaders.

One of the biggest pagan revival movements is *Romuva*, which harkens back to the gods of the sun, water and forests, emphasizing man's oneness with nature. Asked about the Church's concern over the pagan revival, one member of the *Romuva* movement pointed the finger back at the Church, accusing it of the Soviet-style heavy-handedness it had once fought. "Earlier, it was the communists who said they were protecting the state and who made all the people afraid," he said. "Today, it is the Catholic Church that has assumed the task of instilling fear." [34] In 2001, the pagan religious movement *Romuva* wanted to attain the status of a traditional religion. In Lithuania, the religions that have existed for several centuries have such a status, and they also enjoy a sort of support from the State. The fiercest opponent against *Romuva* achieving this status was the Catholic Church.

D. Social Justice and Reconciliation

Church ministering in the transitional times became more difficult. The Church had not only opposed the government, as it had been accustomed to do for centuries,

---

[31] Howard Jarvis, "*A Crisis of Faith*" in *The Baltics Worldwide*, Magazine, Vilnius, 1997, No. 6.
[32] Ibid.
[33] *New Catholic Encyclopedia*, s.v., "France."
[34] Howard Jarvis, "*A Crisis of Faith*."

but in many ways dealt with government leaders while resisting the temptation to cozy up to their power. It required that the Church continually represented those on the margins who are without adequate power or representation. It meant exposing official corruption without regard for consequences, denouncing the use of high office for personal enrichment, and condemning the inevitable acts of cronyism and favoritism that are attendant on all politics. In Lithuania the end of political oppression did not bring to an end economic oppression. It only deepened economic disparities. With each year the new Lithuanian democracy become less and less representative.[35] Business interests overwhelmed parliament and government, corruption became rife, and oligarchies of the rich run the show from behind the scenes.

Unfortunately, the Church contribution to social justice was very limited. One of the reasons for this was the return of Church property that had been confiscated by the Soviets. This became a priority in Church politics. When the Church, during the period of transition, was trying to regain its property, the possibility of discussing social inequality was limited since the Church was dealing with the same government perpetrating the social injustice for the return of its property. The Church never made any official statement against corruption in the government and judicial system.

Soon a formula for collaboration was found between the Church and the State. If the Church supported a political party that was in government, the State would give more money to the Church from the State budget. If the ruling party and the Church were not on good terms, the government threatens not to give money at all. This places another limit on the Church in discussing social justice.

On the county level it is very similar. Many counties have money in their budgets for the Church. It depends on the county officials as to who receives this money. Usually, money is given to those pastors who support the political party that is in power. Knowing this, from the social changes that are happening in society, people in the countryside are suffering more. The government's support is becoming very significant, even more significant than the donations of parishioners. Again, there is no room left to discuss social justice in order to support the poorest and those marginalized within society.

Walter Wink, in his book *When The Powers Fall*, writes:

> One task the churches can undertake as the nation moves toward democracy is to increase the democracy in church structures themselves, the development of more representative and participative styles of church governance, and the repudiation of patriarchy. In many countries, churches

---

[35] Walter Wink, *When the Powers Fall*, 63-64.

cling to traditional authoritarianism, and are a hindrance rather than a help to democratization. It would be a major gift to the world if the churches would at long last condemn domination in all its forms, so that they may more adequately preach and embody Jesus' vision of God's domination-free order.[36]

The editors of *The Chronicle* and the priests who supported them understood the importance of democracy during the Soviet regime. They demanded that in all dioceses priests' councils be allowed to be elected and to help the Church hierarchy run the diocese. It was quite understandable because in this way it would be easier to resist Soviet pressure. *The Chronicle* writes:

> There are disagreements between the hierarchy and the priests on the question of the priests' council. We hear some state that the Holy Father does not approve the existence of councils of priests in Lithuania while others maintain that the only one who does not want councils is the official heading the Office of Religious Affairs. We heard Vatican Radio insist that priests' councils must be set up as soon as possible. That the head official opposes priests' council is confirmed by the words he spoke to one of the bishops: " By permitting the priests council you put a collar on your neck." We are waiting for the Bishops of Lithuania to confirm by secret ballot the priests' councils that have already been elected, councils that by their advice could capably assist the bishops to rule his diocese.[37]

During the times of oppression, in many cases *The Chronicle* spoke a great deal about a more democratic approach in the selection of seminary staff and professors as well as seminarians. When independence was gained, it seems that the Church forgot what they had fought for. When Lithuania became independent, priests' councils did not play a big role in Church leadership, even in those dioceses that are currently being led by former dissidents. The priests' councils are used only to confirm and justify unpopular decisions that need to be made. The very same situation exists in some seminaries. There are no democratic changes. Even some bishops promoted and supported this idea of changing academic titles, as the priests coming back from Rome or finishing in a Lithuanian seminary with a Licentiate of Theology are given the title of Doctor of Theology. This has a negative effect on the

---

[36] Walter Wink, *When the Powers Fall*, 63-64.
[37] *Lietuvos Katalikų Bažnyčios Kronika* (Chronicle of the Catholic Church in Lithuania), Vol. 7, 330-331.

quality of education. Phillip Walton, in studying the Russian Orthodox Church and its consequences after the fall of the Soviet Union, describes it in this way:

> Particular aspects of the Soviet legacy exacerbate the tendency toward schism. Immediately after the end of communism a fundamental problem within the Russian Orthodox Church (and generally in churches throughout Eastern Europe) was that of achieving reconciliation between two groups now divided by bitterness and distrust: those who had "compromised" or "collaborated" with the secular authorities and those who had "resisted" and had been persecuted or discriminated against as a result. The picture was, moreover, complicated by a further consideration. It soon became clear that a basic question needed to be asked about any religious believer who had resisted the communist system: had he or she done so because that system was totalitarian or because it was atheist? An individual in the former category would now, in the post communist period, very likely be found in the camp promoting democratization, pluralism, and freedom of conscience for all. An individual in the latter category, by contrast, would in the post communist period tend to be defensive of the "truth," conservative, triumphalist, and intolerant of innovations in the spiritual sphere.[38]

We can arrive at the same conclusions as Phillip Walter, especially as they apply to the dissidents who are not yet reconciled. They did not defend a process of democracy within society. Usually, they are defending their own truth and they are short on tolerance towards those who have differing opinions and foster the process of democratization in society. In some cases it is possible to say that the oppressed has become the oppressor. It is because in all their lives they experienced only two models of action: to be oppressed or to oppress others. Soon it became evident that to deal with priests who had been collaborators was easier than with those who had not been involved with the fight, but quietly worked for the Church, bringing the spirit of Vatican II to the communities where they served as pastors, as well as liberating those communities from a totalitarian mentality. The former dissidents who are now in power do not respect those priests. They left in place many who had collaborated. It is easier to deal with them because for decades they were loyal to the KGB structures. Now they appeared to be loyal to Church leaders. Even though they have new

---

[38] Philip Walters, "The Russian Orthodox Church and Foreign Christianity the Legacy of the Past" in John Witte Jr. and Michael Bourdeaux (ed), *Proselytism and Orthodoxy in Russia,* 46-47.

superiors their mentality remains the same. In this way, they continue the authoritarian leadership in the Church. The spirit of Vatican II and the changes in society require greater involvement and the sharing of responsibilities with the lay ministry in the Church. Unfortunately, this did not happen. In many parishes, parish councils do not exist at all. In some cases, these councils exist only on paper. Only the clergy controls leadership and finances.

This situation helped the post-totalitarian mentality to flourish. This comprises contradictory elements. On the one hand, it includes the tendency to expect solutions from strong leaders rather than from personal initiative, and the tendency to dramatize oneself as the impotent victim of uncontrollable circumstances ("learned helplessness"). On the other hand, the individual in power may see himself or herself as the measure of all things, showing a tendency to seek maximum solutions and to regard compromise as suspect and dishonorable – "if you disagree with me you are not only mistaken but a scoundrel"-and a tendency to identify personal opinion with absolute truth. The contradictory elements in the post-totalitarian mentality tend toward polarization among those who are faced with the message the churches are trying to bring. While some are extremely skeptical and suspicious of any attempt to replace the old compulsory truths with a new set, however different in content these may be, others eagerly embrace the Christian message as a new set of truths to be adhered to as unquestioningly as the old communist ideology. Many former collaborators and unreconciled dissidents are often among the most xenophobic and isolationist of Church members, bringing over wholesale into their new faith the conviction nurtured in them in communist times when they were surrounded by enemies and needed constantly to be vigilant and unmask them.[39]

Another problem to keep in mind when talking about post-communist society is the question of who is a victim and who is a perpetrator. In Argentina or Chile it was tragically clear when the victim "disappeared" or was tortured by the military, or death squads. In Soviet Lithuania, in one case a person might be the perpetrator in one setting or time period, and victim in another, as in the case of Church administrator Jokubauskas, who at first collaborated. Then, when Soviet authorities found him useless, they killed him.[40] In post-communist Lithuania it is more complicated. Many passive collaborators and even active collaborators are unwilling to repent. Many of them feel that what they did was necessary for the salvation of the Church and the country and that they are therefore not culpable. The official position of the Catholic

---

[39] Philip Walters, "The Russian Orthodox Church and Foreign Christianity the Legacy of the Past" in John Witte Jr. and Michael Bourdeaux (ed), *Proselytism and Orthodoxy in Russia*, 47.
[40] *Lietuvos Ypatingasis Archyvas* (The Special Archives of Lithuania - KGB files), Vilnius, file K-1, folder 14, b59, 17-19 (15,16 destroyed).

Church of Lithuania of "forgive and forget" favors them as well.

At first, it seemed that the biggest problem was the collaborators; but when looking at things more deeply, we can see that there are problems on the side of the former dissidents, with the exception of a few who live in the spirit of reconciliation.

Many dissidents said that they forgive their wrongdoers, but their theological knowledge of reconciliation is limited, and they have no interest in seeking such reconciliation. Reconciliation is more than forgiveness, however. Forgiveness can be unilateral; reconciliation is always mutual. One can forgive those who are not even aware that one has something against them. The goal of forgiveness is always reconciliation. Reconciliation means reestablishing love between two estranged parties. Sometimes forgiveness for its own sake is selfish, narcissistic, and private.[41] Another difficulty of seeking reconciliation within the Church is that many stopped at forgiveness and only a few thought about reconciliation. From the same dissidents it sounded as if to forgive is to admit weakness and to be humiliated again in the face of wrongdoers.

If dissidents are talking about reconciliation, they understand that reconciliation should go in this way: first, repentance from the wrongdoer's side, then follows forgiveness from the victim, and then both sides reconcile. But from the Christian perspective, where God leads reconciliation, the process begins with the victim, the sequence is reconciliation followed by forgiveness and then repentance from the wrongdoer's side. Only a few of the former dissidents are familiar with and living according to the Christian strategy of reconciliation.

The Lithuanian Church can be proud of what it did during the time of oppression. It was like the Church in Chile during the time of a military junta when the Church bravely resisted the military regime. But in Lithuania, oppression and the Soviet regime lasted many decades. During that period, the KGB managed to weaken the Church's spirit, infiltrating collaborators and wrongdoers into Church circles, implementing their own moral norms in the Church.

When the country regained its independence, the Church had already been weakened and did not act according to the theology of reconciliation. In this way the Church could not participate in the processes of reconciliation within the society. During the last decades there are only a few things that the Church can be proud of because the Church did not adapt itself to the social changes that occurred in society. The Church did not apologize for those members who had collaborated and the activities of the Church after independence became similar to those of the Church in Argentina. When the military junta had gone, the Church in Argentina was unable to

---

[41] Walter Wink, *When the Powers Fall*, 16.

find the strength to tell the truth about what had happened and failed miserably in the process of reconciliation.

The Lithuanian government was different from General DeGaulle of France because it never demanded that the collaborators be removed from office. This is understandable because the Lithuanian government had to be created from nothing. In this case, the State could not help the Church in the process of reconciliation as had happened in post World War II France. This situation is similar to the fourth century Donatist controversy. In some dioceses, for as long as a decade, leadership positions were in the hands of the collaborators.

The above analysis points to the fact that repressing the truth through a willingness to embark upon a new period in the country's history was the wrong move. This position did not take into consideration the fundamental human need for justice and the desire for both moral and material compensation for previous suffering. The repression of truth telling cannot lead to true reconciliation.

Repressing the truth was a great obstacle to unity in the Church. Technically speaking, there is only one Roman Catholic Church in Lithuania, but a careful analysis of the Church-sponsored and Church–affiliated media makes it very clear that they are two quite different currents within the Church itself. One can differentiate between the traditional attitudes of the Lithuanian weekly *XXI Amžius*[42] *(The XXIst Century)*. This faction can be characterized as presenting strong defensive attitudes toward the changes that are taking place in Lithuania, easily creating enemies among the people as well as among institutions. Their concept of God represents him as vengeful and vindictive. Their piety is based upon criticism of this world. This position makes a virtue of the constant search for 'heretics' and condemnation of all people who do not subscribe to the ideas maintained by the group.

Another group runs the radio station *Mažoji Studija* and magazine *Naujasis Židinys*.[43] It is possible to briefly characterize this group as presenting a realistic evaluation of the current situation, its dangers as well as its strengths. This group stressed that the Church would be more of a Church if it left all the places it needed to take during communism, and restrict its own activity to pastoral work. The Church is not needed to intervene between the state and the people any longer. The Lithuanian hierarchy often criticizes this group and in many cases favors the first. A great number of former dissidents, with few exceptions, support the first group as well.

---

[42] A Lithuanian Catholic newspaper published in Lithuania since 1990.
[43] A Lithuanian Catholic magazine published in Lithuania since 1991.

IN CONCLUSION:
CAN THE CHURCH OF TODAY CONTRIBUTE
TO THE PROCESS OF RECONCILIATION?

Despite all the difficulties and obstacles, the Church should contribute to the process of reconciliation within the Church and society because the Church's mission flows from the Bible. The message in the Bible is very clear in terms of reconciliation. These days there is an extreme need to seek social reconciliation, to reconstruct social order in society, especially between the rich and the poor of society. There is a large gap between those two groups. During the last years of Soviet rule, almost everyone was economically equal. One decade later, the wealthiest ten percent spend 8.3 times more than the poorest ten percent of the population, according to UN human resources statistics.[44] Keeping in mind that the poor spend all of their income and the wealthiest spend only a portion, while investing the rest or using their income in other ways, we see what a large discrepancy has developed between these two strata of society. This discrepancy is growing, as are tension and discontent.

In 1995, the bishops of Poland, having understood the complexity of the antagonistic bondage of the Soviet system, and being in the process of disentangling themselves from it, released a pastoral letter:

> One of the conditions for a real dialog is the necessity of rediscovering all the painful truths about the past of communist rule. The Church stresses that it is necessary to learn about truth and bring to public attention all misdeeds, but at the same time, avoid a "witch hunt." What is important is to publicly present what some people have done, ask them to admit what they have done, compensate the victims, and only afterwards, forgive them. We hope that the fact that we reflect on painful events from the most contemporary history of Poland will not create attitudes of hate, revenge and contempt. It is the Christian tradition of Poland that we are capable to say "we forgive," but in order

---

[44] Jolanta Rimkutė and Edita Vološčiuk (ed), *Pranešimas apie žmogaus socialinę raidą Lietuvoje 2001*, 21.

to do so, a basic condition needs to be fulfilled: the wrong deeds need to be admitted and readiness to compensate for wrong deeds to the extent it is possible now have to be expressed. Dialogue and responsibility allow the honest analysis of the past, which will not create new harm and hate but will help to build a future on a stable foundation without false or unspoken things.[45]

The Polish Catholic Church is trying to seek reconciliation. Bishops of the Lithuanian Catholic Church are still silent. In order to contribute to the process of social reconciliation, Church members need to study the theology and the spirituality of reconciliation. It is a big challenge for those who were dissidents. If they do not achieve individual reconciliation and see things in a new light, contribution of the Church to social reconciliation will not be possible.

Robert Schreiter says that there are three resources in particular which the Church should bring to the process of reconciliation: " The first is its message about reconciliation and the spirituality that flows out of it. The second is the power of its rituals. And the third is its capacity to create communities of reconciliation."[46]

A. Theology of Reconciliation and the Spirituality that Flows out of it.

Even though the Church did not act according to the spirit of reconciliation, the Church authority is still very influential. For this reason one can say that, in theory, the Church could contribute to the reconciliation of society. That is, if members of the Church understood the importance of the mission of Christian reconciliation, the deepest essence and meaning of which are contained in the following words of the apostle Paul:

> So if anyone is in Christ, there is a new creation: everything has become new! All this is from God, who reconciled us to himself through Christ, and has given us the ministry of reconciliation; that is, in Christ God was reconciling the world to himself, not counting their trespasses against them, and entrusting the message of reconciliation to us. So we are ambassadors for Christ, since God is making his appeal through us; we entreat you on behalf of Christ, be reconciled to God. (2 Cor. 5: 17-20)

---

[45] Pastoral Letter of Polish Bishops, October 1995.
[46] Robert Schreiter, *The Ministry of Reconciliation: Spirituality and Strategies* (Maryknoll, NY: Orbis Books, 1998), 127.

Even the third chapter of this study was devoted to the theology and the spirituality of reconciliation.

Following are a few more thoughts pertinent to the situation of the Catholic Church in Lithuania: The experience of reconciliation makes both the victim and the wrongdoer "a new creation." (2 Corinthians 5:17) Strategies of reconciliation often aim at getting a society back to the state it was in prior to the conflict. But the sheer enormity of what happened—"not less than 456,000 people fell victim to Soviet genocide and terror (every third adult),"[47] infiltration of KGB agents into all spheres of life, especially the Catholic Church, and the social changes that took place in a country during Soviet isolation—make such a return to a prior condition virtually impossible.

Christians believe that the reconciliation that God works is not a restoration to a former state, but a situation in which both victim and evildoers are taken to a new place. The victims, having experienced reconciliation, no longer demand vengeance upon the wrongdoers, but are able to imagine a totally new state of affairs. *In order to achieve a 'new place' Church leaders must change their strategy:*

1. **Studying the teaching of Vatican II among members of the clergy, among students in the Catholic seminaries and later on among lay members of the Church.**
2. **Greater openness on the side of clergy towards lay members of the Church, accepting them as independent subjects in the Church not only as objects of pastoral care.**
3. **To study and to live according to the theology of reconciliation, according to the Gospel.**
4. **To identify not only with the wealthy class, but also to exercise clear support of social justice while not limiting oneself to charitable works.**
5. **Particular emphasis on the youth, requiring a more modern approach to evangelization that is better suited to their needs.**
6. **Openness of the Church towards people who are not necessarily Church members, preventing divisions between 'us' and 'them.'**
7. **Retaining independence from political authorities, acting without the support of political institutions.**

---

[47] Arvydas Anušauskas, *Lietuvių Tautos Sovietinia Naikinimas 1940 – 1958* (The Soviet Destruction of Lithuanian Nation 1940 – 1958), Vilnius: Vaga, 1996, 469-470.

Here one enters the difficult areas of justice and forgiveness. We know that justice - in the sense of restitution - is sometimes impossible to achieve (as in the case of justice for the dead). Punishment of wrongdoers may not achieve anything like an equivalent for the evil that has been done. Similarly, forgiveness can never be simply the restoration of the old way of doing things.

A mark of the Christian understanding of reconciliation is precisely this "new creation," namely, that God leads both victims and wrongdoers to new life in the future that gets beyond the undeniable hurt of the past. What creates this new humanity for victims and wrongdoers can be found in the story of the passion, death and resurrection of Jesus Christ. Christians believe that the reconciliation that God has worked for has been brought about through the suffering, death, and resurrection of Jesus Christ, delivering us from the evil that afflicts our world. There are two distinct ideas that are important here.

First, the Catholic theology of reconciliation says that Jesus' unjust and violent suffering and death are the ways that the structure of power and evil in the world are overcome. In that suffering and death, Jesus has taken on the power of evil and has overcome it. The resurrection can be seen as a paradigm of reconciliation: the risen Jesus is the reconciled new creation, the source of reconciliation for every victim of power and evil in our world. God overcomes evil not by ignoring or dismissing it, but by entering into it so as to conquer it from the inside.

Second, the story of Jesus' unjust suffering and death becomes a "dangerous memory" for Christians and indeed for the whole world. That memory means that no evil will ever be allowed to prevail, no matter how heinous. The reconciling power of the God of life is always stronger, and can always bring victims through that experience to a new creation. As a result, Christians discover ways of placing their own story of suffering inside the bigger story of the suffering and death of Christ in order to overcome its effects. In the words of Paul, "I want to know Christ and the power of his resurrection and the sharing of his sufferings by becoming like him in his death." (Philippians 3: 10)

The Christian understanding of reconciliation reveals a deeper truth about the idle world itself. Christians believe that this understanding of reconciliation as the work of God in Christ for the sake of the world reveals a number of things about the world. First of all, it takes seriously just how complexly and how deeply evil and wrongdoing permeate the world. It took the suffering and death of the very Son of God to overcome it. As a result, even though Christians believe that reconciliation is first and foremost the work of God, this never leads them to a passive stance toward the work of reconciliation. Their active struggle to bring about reconciliation reflects God's own commitment to the world and to the victims of evil.

Third, the cross of Christ stands as a paradoxical symbol of how God overcomes the evil of the world. At the time of Christ it was a symbol of utter humiliation and (for the powerful) the betrayal of State power. It was "a stumbling block for Jews and foolishness to the Greeks." (1 Corinthians 1:25) But it reveals a deeper meaning of where power *does* lie: with the Creator and with those whom the Creator loves, even though they may be considered weak, powerless and foolish to the world.[48]

If the Church wishes to be an authentic bearer of the Gospel of Christ, then it cannot afford to ignore the invitation for reconciliation that flows from the Gospel recounting the suffering of Christ and the Resurrection. Through living in the spirit of reconciliation the need arises for rituals of reconciliation and communities of reconciliation.

B. Power of the rituals and communities of reconciliation

The first official ritual of reconciliation was celebrated during the millennium celebration when the Vatican invited all the local churches to have a liturgy of reconciliation. From those days ecumenical services were organized at an official Church level. The rituals and communities of reconciliation spring from the theology of reconciliation as well as the spirituality that comes with it, and are not merely handed down from above. The Catholic Church in Lithuania has not achieved much in this area. Many identify confession with the ritual of reconciliation. In a social situation of conflict and injustices it becomes clear that the sacrament of reconciliation administered by the ordinary ministers may not be suitable. Some Church ministries in the Lithuanian situation sided with the wrongdoer. Ministers of the Church must earn the right to be ministers of reconciliation. If one was a dissident, one must first reconcile with the past. If one was a wrongdoer or profited from the Soviet regime, in a moral sense he should not be active in social reconciliation but rather seek repentance. The younger generation of priests who began their service early on must earn the trust of the victims in order to act as mediators of reconciliation.

There is a need to create communities of reconciliation and at the parish level. In many parishes there are tensions between those parishioners who were loyal and who remained part of the Church during the persecution and those who distanced themselves from the Church during the persecution and who now want to return to the Church. Some priests who have a spirit of reconciliation are instrumental in uniting these two groups. Where there is a lack of this spirit, the parishes are experiencing tensions.

---

[48] Brian Starken (ed), *Working for Reconciliation A Caritas Handbook*, 34-35.

But for many young people the first experience about rituals and communities of reconciliation was the spirit of the Taizé community. A few thousand young Lithuanians every year have participated in the liturgy and prayers for reconciliation in the village of Taizé or during European gatherings in major European cities at Christmas break. The Taizé community has a powerful story of reconciliation.

Taizé began with one man, Brother Roger. In 1940, he arrived at what was then a semi-abandoned village in Burgundy. He was 25 years old, and he had gone there to offer shelter to political refugees, notably Jews fleeing the Nazi persecution, and to work out a call to follow Christ in a community, a community that would attempt to live the Gospel call to reconciliation day after day. The autumn of 1944 brought liberation to France. The first years after the war were difficult. The local population had never been very understanding, and the welcome the brothers offered to German prisoners did not make their life any easier. Poverty was rife and the temptation to move elsewhere must have been a strong one.

Upon the liberation of France, Roger and his three prospective brothers moved to a house in Taizé with the conviction that they must continue the venture of having amongst them "those who were most bereft." Who, however, would be the most bereft in the human desert where they were to settle? The answer was presented to them when it was decided that German prisoners of war should be installed in the abandoned villages very close to Taizé: some at Mont, others in a former youth camp near Chazelles. The small community obtained permission to visit prisoners-of-war and there they discovered that those in charge of German prisoners were in terms of their humanity "the poorest of the poor."[49]

The plight of the occupants of the camps touched the young men at Taizé deeply. They shared with the afflicted prisoners the little food that was available at the time, and on Sundays they were permitted to receive a number of them at the house for a meal and a brief moment of prayer. To have known the two situations, that of the political refugees, those who were hiding, those who were seeking refuge, and then very shortly afterwards that of the German prisoners of war who were "just as innocent as the first," remains for Brother Roger a powerful experience. His sympathy and compassion were not, however, shared by all of the local population.

Some of the men from the area surrounding Taizé who belonged to the Resistance had never returned from their secret activities. There were feelings of vengeance on the part of two or three of the women, and hatred engendered hatred. One day some of the women whose husbands had been deported and had died in German concentration camps set upon one young prisoner with leather harnesses used for cattle. Weak and undernourished as he was, he died from the beating, but he was a

---

[49] Brother Roger, *The Taizé Experience* (Collegeville, Minesota: The Liturgical Press, 1990), 78.

144

priest and in his last hours he expressed only peace and forgiveness. "For some time I had noticed in him a reflection of the sanctity of God," recalls Brother Roger.[50]

Brother Roger is a living example for many young Catholics in Europe and in Lithuania. His life confirms that reconciliation is not merely a task to be achieved. For those who are reconciled, reconciliation becomes a calling. They move to a wholly new place, from which they call oppressors to repentance and serve in a prophetic way for the whole society.

How much hatred is often directed at those who extend a hand of reconciliation in the Church of Lithuania! Even Cardinal Vincentas Sladkevičius, who extended invitations for reconciliation and knew how to conduct dialogues with representatives of a post-communist world, was often called "Cardinal of the Reds" (similar to Brother Roger's being called a "Nazi collaborator"). His life could serve as an example of a man who achieved the spirit of reconciliation in spite of the persecution he had suffered. He lived in that spirit and invited Lithuanian society to seek reconciliation. This fact is reflected in his life from the moment Independence was regained. In 1988, when the still-ruling Communist Party returned the Vilnius Cathedral, which had been used as an art gallery, to the Catholics the Cardinal made no rebuke or reproach, but merely thanked the gallery director for having preserved the Cathedral so beautifully; and during his sermon the Cardinal invited the nation to reconciliation:

> My dear people let us learn how to wait; let us learn how to be patient; let us learn not to step on the heels of one another. Let us learn not to push one another around and keep from hurting one another. For change of the season shoots, planted in the fall, spring and summer will arrive, bringing to our nation a harvest of change, promising a blessed future. My dear people, it is necessary for us to know not only how to wait patiently but also how to grow like shoots. A shoot will grow in the spring; the ears will flow out, and the first grains will appear in the ears. Dearly beloved, to wait means to grow and our nation must join its waiting with growth. The way we should grow is beautifully pointed out in the Gospel of Christ which tells us about the Child Jesus who grew "in wisdom, age, and grace before God and men." (Lk.2, 52)[51]

---

[50] Kathryn Spink, *A Universal Heart* (San Francisco: Harper & Row, 1987), 49-51.
[51] Irena Petraitienė, *Kardinolas* (Kaunas, Lithuania: Santara, 2000), 98.

BIBLIOGRAPHY

A. Books

Aitmatov, Chingiz. *The Day Lasts More than a Hundred Years*. Bloomington, IN: University Press, 1988.

Anušauskas, Arvydas. *Lietuvių Tautos Sovietinia Naikinimas 1940 – 1958* (The Soviet Destruction of Lithuanian Nation 1940 – 1958). Vilnius: Vaga, 1996.

Anušauskas, Arvydas (ed.) *The Anti-Soviet Resistance in the Baltic States*. Vilnius:Genocide and Resistance Research Center of Lithuania, 1999.

Bagdonavičius, Vytautas (ed.) *Arkivyskupas Mečislovas Reinys*. Chicago: Lietuvių Krikščionių Demokratų Sąjunga, 1977.

Baum, Gregory & Wells, Harold. *The Reconciliation of Peoples: a Challenge to the Church*. Maryknoll, N.Y: Orbis Books, 1997.

Bernard, Russell. *Research Methods in Anthropology*. Thousand Oaks, CA: Sage Publications, 1994.

Boraine, Alex, Levy, Janet & Scheffer, Ronel. *Dealing with the Past: Truth and Reconciliation in South Africa*. Cape Town: IDASA, 1994.

Bosch, David J. *Transforming Mission*. Maryknoll, N Y: Orbis Books, 1991.

Botman, H. & Petersen, Robin M. *To Remember and to Heal: Theological and Psychological Reflections on Truth and Reconciliation*. Cape Town: Human & Rousseau, 1996.

Bourdeaux, Michael. *Land of Crosses*. Devon: Augustine Publishing Company, 1979.

Bronkhorst, Daan. *Truth and Reconciliation: Obstacles and Opportunities for Human Rights*. Amsterdam: Amnesty International Dutch Section, 1995.

Brother Roger, *The Taizé Experience*. Collegville, MN: The Liturgical Press, 1990.

The Catholic Encyclopedia. New York: McGraw-Hill Book Company, 1965.

Cavanaugh, William T. *Torture and Eucharist*. Oxford: Blackwell Publishers, 1998.

The Chronicle of the Catholic Church in Lithuania 1972-74. Chicago: Loyola University Press, Vol. 1., 1978.

The Chronicle of the Catholic Church in Lithuania 1979-81. Chicago: The Society of the Chronicle of Lithuania, Vol. 6.,1989.

147

The Chronicle of the Catholic Church in Lithuania vol. 28. New York: Lithuanian R.C. Priests' League of America, 1978.

The Chronicle of the Catholic Church in Lithuania vols. 1-10. Lithuanian Catholic Religious Aid Auxiliary Society, Chicago, 1987.

Corcoran, John Anthony. *Augustinus Contra Donatistas*. Donaldson, Indiana: Graduate Theological Foundation, 1997.

Cross, F.I. *The Oxford Dictionary of the Christian Church*. Oxford: Oxford University Press, 1988.

Developing Countries. 4 vols. Boulder: Lynne Rienner Publishers, 1990.

Diamond, Larry Juan, Linz, J. & Lipset. Seymour Martin. *Democracy in Theory, Research, and Practice*. New York: Guilford, 2000.

Drapac, Vesna. *War and Religion Catholics in the Churches of Occupied Paris*. Washington, D C: The Catholic University of America Press, 1998.

Dwyer, John C. *Church History*. New York: Paulist Press, 1985.

Elliot, Lawrence. *I will be Called John*. New York: Readers Digest Press, 1973.

Encyclopedia Lituanica: Boston, MA: Lithuanian Encyclopedia Press, 1975.

Enright, Robert & North, Joanna (eds.) *Exploring Forgiveness*. Madison, WI: University of Wisconsin Press, 1998.

Fleet, Michael & Smith, Brian H. *The Catholic Church and Democracy in Chile and Peru*. South Bend, IN: University of Notre Dame Press, 1997.

Gittins, Anthony. *Observant Participation: Ethics, " Hard Words," and Liturgical Inculturation*. Collegeville, MN: The Liturgical Press, 1996.

Hammersley, Martyn & Atkinson, Paul. *Ethnography: Principles and Practice*. London:Oxford Press, 1995.

Halls, W.D. *Politics, Society and Christianity in Vichy, France*. Oxford: Berg Publishers, 1995.

Havel, Vaclav. *Power of the Powerless*. London: Hutchison, 1985.

Herman, Judith. *Trauma and Recovery*. New York: Basic Books, 1992.

Hurley, Michael, S.J. *Reconciliation in Religion and Society: Proceedings of a Conference Organized by the Irish School of Ecumenics at the University of Ulster*. Belfast: Institute of Irish Studies, Queens University, 1994.

Ignatavičius, Idzidorius. *Lietuvos Naikinimas ir Tautos Kova 1940 – 1998*. Vilnius: Vaga,1999.

Ivereigh, Austen. *Catholicism and Politics in Argentina: 1810-1960*. Oxford: St. Martin's Press, 1995.

Ivinskis, Zenonas. *Rinktiniai raštai*. Rome: Lietuvių Katalikų Mokslo Akademija, 1987.

Jenco, Lawrence Martin, O.S.M. *Bound to Forgive: The Pilgrimage to Reconciliation of a Beirut Hostage*. South Bend, IN: Ave Maria Press, 1995.

Jones, L. Gregory. *Embodying Forgiveness: A Theological Analysis*. Grand Rapids, MI: Wm. B. Eerdmans, 1995.

The Kairos Document: Challenge to the Church. Braamfontein: The Kairos Theologians, 1985.

Kelman, Herbert C., & D. P. Warwick. *The Ethics of Social Intervention*. Washington, D.C.: Halstead Press, 1978.

KGB Archives. Genocide and Resistance Research Center of Lithuania in Vilnius, Lithuania.

Kim, Syoon. "God Reconciled His Enemy to Himself: The Origins of Paul's Concept of Reconciliation" in *The Road from Damascus*. Longnecker, R.N. (ed.) Grand Rapids, MI: Edermans, 1992.

Kritz, Neil J. *Transitional Justice: How Emerging Democracies Reckon with Former Regimes*, 3 Vols. Washington, DC: United States Institute of Peace, 1995.

Kung, Hans. *Global Responsibility: In Search of a New World Ethic*. New York: Crossroads, 1991.

Lakey, George. *Powerful Peacemaking: A Strategy for a Living Revolution*. Philadelphia: New Society Publishers, 1987.

Lederach, John Paul. *The Journey Toward Reconciliation*. Scottsdale, PA: Herald Press, 1999.

Lederach, John Paul. *Building Peace: Sustainable Reconciliation in Divided Societies*. Washington, DC: United States Institute of Peace, 1997

Lerner, Michael. *Surplus Powerlessness*. London: Humanities Press International, 1986.

Lietuvių Archyvas (Lithuanian Archive), Kaunas, Lithuania 1942.

Lietuvos Katalikų Bažnyčios Kronika 1974-1975. Vol. 2 (*Chronicle of the Catholic Church in Lithuania*). Chicago: Lithuanian Catholic Religious Aid Supporters, 1975.

Lietuvos Katalikų Bažnyčios Kronika. Vol.5. (Chronicle of the Catholic Church in Lithuania). Chicago: The Society of the Chronicle of Lithuania, 1979.

Lietuvos Katalikų Bažnyčios Kronika 1981-83. Vol. 7 (Chronicle of the Catholic Church in Lithuania). Chicago: The Society of the Chronicle of Lithuania, 1984.

Lietuvos Katalikų Bažnyčios Kronika 1983-85. Vol. 8 (*Chronicle of the Catholic Church in Lithuania*). Chicago: The Society of the Chronicle of Lithuania,1987.

Lietuvos Katalikų Bažnyčios Kronika 1985-87. Vol. 9 (Chronicle of the Catholic Church in Lithuania). Chicago: The Society of the Chronicle of Lithuania, 1989.

Lietuvos Katalikų Bažnyčios Kronika 1987-88. Vol.10 (Chronicle of the Catholic Church in Lithuania). Chicago: The Society of the Chronicle of Lithuania, 1992.

Lietuvos Vyskupai Kankiniai Sovietiniame Teisme. (*Lithuanian Bishop Martyrs Under Soviet Rule*). Vilnius: The Lithuanian Catholic Academy of Science, 2000.

Lietuvos Vyskupų Konferencijos 2000metu Jubiliejaus komitetas, *Atgailos ir Atsiprašymo pamaldų intencijos ir maldos*. 14 April 2000.

Lietuvos Ypatingasis Archyvas. (The Special Archives of Lithuania - KGB files) Vilnius.

Linden, Ian. *The Catholic Church and the Struggle for Zimbabwe*. London: Longman, 1980.

Lofgren, Joan. "Reconciliation in the Soviet Past" in McSpadden, Liucia Ann (ed.) *Reaching Reconciliation*. Uppsala, Sweden: Life & Peace Institute, 2000.

Logue, Judy. *Forgiving the People You Love to Hate*. Ligouri, MO: Ligouri Press, 1997.

Lopez, George, & Stohl, Michael. *Liberalization and Redemocratization in Latin America*. New York: Greenwood Press, 1987.

Malamud-Goti, Jaime. "Trying Violators of Human Rights: The Dilemma of Transitional Democratic Governments." *State Crimes: Punishment or Pardon*. Queenstown, MD: The Justice and Society Program of Aspen Institute, 1988.

McBrien, Richard P. *Catholicism*. Minneapolis: Winston Press, 1966.

McBrien, Richard P. *Lives of the Popes*. San Francisco: Harper San Francisco, 2000.

McCullough, Michael, Pargament, Kenneth & Thoresen, Carl (eds.) *Forgiveness: Theory, Research, and Practice*. New York: Guilford, 2000.

McSorley, Richard. *The New Testament Basis of Peacemaking*. Scottsdale, PA: Herald Press, 1979.

McSpadden, Liucia Ann (ed.) *Reaching Reconciliation*. Uppsala, Sweden: Life & Peace Institute, 2000.

Merton, Thomas. *Faith and Violence*. South Bend, IN: University of Notre Dame Press, 1965.

Mignone, Emilio F. *Witness to the Truth: The Complicity of Church and Dictatorship in Argentina 1976-1983*. Maryknoll, N.Y: Orbis Books 1988.

Miller, Allen O. *A Christian Declaration on Human Rights*. Grand Rapids, MI: Wm. B. Eerdmans, 1977.

Miller-Fahrenholz, Geiko. *The Art of Forgiveness*. Geneva: WCC Publications, 1997.

Mitchell, Margaret M. *Paul and the Rhetoric of Reconciliation*. Westminster: John Knox Press,1989.

Muller, Alois, & Greinacher, Norbert. *The Church and the Rights of Man*. New York: Seabury Press, 1979.

Murphy, Jeffrie G., & Hampton, Jean. *Forgiveness and Mercy*. Cambridge: Cambridge University Press, 1988.

Musto, Ronald G. *The Catholic Peace Tradition*. Maryknoll, N.Y: Orbis Books, 1986.

New Catholic Encyclopedia, Washington: McGraw-Hill Book Company, 1989.

Nielsen, Niels C. *Revolutions in Eastern Europe: The Religious Roots*. Maryknoll, N.Y: Orbis Books, 1991.

O'Brien, Niall. *Island of Tears, Island of Hope*. Maryknoll, N.Y.: Orbis Books, 1993.

O'Brien, N. *Revolution from the Heart*. New York: Oxford University Press, 1987.

Paltarokas, Kazimieras. *Katalikų Tikybos Katekizmas*. Kaunas: Žemaičių vyskupija. 1913.

Paltarokas, Kazimieras, *Trumpas Katalikų Katekizmas*. Kaunas: XXI amžius, 1999.

Paul, Harry W. *The Second Relliement: The Rapprochement Between Church an State in France in the Twentieth Century*. Washington, DC: The Catholic University of America Press, 1967.

Petraitienė, Irena. *Kardinolas*. Kaunas: Santara, 2000.

Preston, Ronald H. *Church and Society in the Late Twentieth Century: The Economic and Political Task*. London: SCM Press, 1963.

Prunskis, Juozas. Lietuva bolševikų okupacijoje (Lithuanian Occupied by the Soviet Union). Chicago: Jūrų Šaulių Kupoa Klaipėda, 1979.

Ravitch, Notman. *The Catholic Church and the French Nation 1589-1989*. London: Routledge, 1990.

Remeikis, Tomas. *The Violations of Human Rights in Soviet Lithuania: A Report for 1978*. Glenside, PA: The Lithuanian American Community, 1979.

Remeikis, Tomas. *The Violations of Human Rights in Soviet Lithuania: A Report for 1981*. Glenside, PA: The Lithuanian American Community, 1982.

Rosenbloom, Dena & Williams, Mary Beth. *Life after Trauma: A Workbook for Healing*. New York: Guilford, 1999.

Rimkutė, Jolanta & Vološčiuk, Edita (eds.). *Pranešimas apie žmogaus socialinę raidą Lietuvoje 2001*. Vilnius: Jungtinių Tautų vystymo programa, 2001.

Russell, Bernard. *Research Methods in Anthropology*. Thousand Oaks, CA: Sage Publications, 1995.

Salmi, Jamil. *Violence & Democratic Society: New Approaches to Human Rights*. London: ZED Books, 1993.

Savasis, J. *The War Against God in Lithuania*. New York: Manyland Books, 1966.

Schreiter, Robert. *Reconciliation: Mission and Ministry in a Changing Social Order*. Maryknoll, NY: Orbis Books, 1992.

Schreiter, Robert. The Ministry of Reconciliation: Spirituality and Strategies. Maryknoll, NY: Orbis Books, 1998.

Senn, Alfred Erich. *Lithuania Awakening.* Los Angeles: University of California Press, 1990.

Shenk, Gerald. *God With Us? The Roles of Religion in the Former Yugoslavia.* Uppsala: Life & Peace Institute, 1993.

Shriver, Donald. *An Ethic for Enemies.* New York: Oxford University Press, 1995.

Skabeikis, Marian (ed.). *Catholics in Soviet- Occupied Lithuania.* Brooklyn, NY: Lithuanian Catholic Religious Aid, 1981.

Smith, Brian H. *The Church and Politics in Chile.* Princeton, NJ: Princeton University Press, 1982.

Spengla, Vidas. "Akiplėša," KGB file on Rev. Juozas Zdebskis. Vilnius: Lumen, 1996.

Spink, Kathryn. *A Universal Heart.* San Francisco: Harper & Row, 1987.

Starken, Brian (ed.). *Working for Reconciliation: A Caritas Handbook.* Vatican City: Caritas Internationalis, 1999.

Suziedelis, Saulius. *The Sword and the Cross.* Huntington, IN: Our Sunday Visitor Publishing Division, 1988.

Swettenham, John Alexander. *The Tragedy of the Baltic States.* New York: Frederick A. Praeger, 1954.

Tauras, K. V. *Guerilla Warfare on the Amber Coast.* New York: Voyages Press, 1962.

Tavuchis, Nicholas. *Mea Culpa: A Sociology of Apology and Reconciliation.* Stanford: Stanford University Press, 1991.

Thistlethwaite. Susan. *A Just Peace Church.* New York: United Church Press, 1986.

Tischner, Jose E. *The Spirit of Solidarity.* San Francisco: Harper & RDYO, 1984.

Tooke, John. *The Cost of Reconciliation in South Africa.* Cape Town: Methodist Publishing House, 1988.

Tutu, Desmond Mpilo. *No Future Without Forgiveness.* New York: Doubleday, 1999.

Vaišnora, J. *Marijos Garbinimas Lietuvoje.* Rome: Lietuvių Katalikų Mokslo Akademija, 1958.

Vardys, Stanley. *Lithuania Under the Soviets.* New York: Frederick A. Praeger, 1965.

Vardys, Stanley. *The Catholic Church: Dissent and Nationality in Soviet Lithuania.* New York: Columbia University Press, 1978.

Vedomosty Verkhovnogo Soveta Sovetskih Socialisticheshikh Respublik, Moscow, 1968.

Villa-Vicencio, Charles. *A Theology of Reconstruction: Nation-Building and Human Rights.* Cambridge: Cambridge University Press, 1992.

Volf, Miroslav. Exclusion and Embrace: A Theological Exploration of Identity, Otherness, and Reconciliation. Nashville: Abingdon Press 1996.

Walters, Philip. "The Russian Orthodox Church and Foreign Christianity: The Legacy of the Past" in Witte Jr., John & Bourdeaux, Michael (eds). *Proselytism and Orthodoxy in Russia*. Maryknoll, New York: Orbis Books, 1999.

White, James F. *A Brief History of Christian Worship*. Nashville: Abigdon Press, 1993.

Whitehead, James D. & Whitehead, Evelyn Eaton. *Method in Ministry*. Kansas City: Sheed & Ward, 1995.

Wink, Walter. *When the Powers Fall*. Minneapolis: Fortress Press, 1998.

B. Periodicals and Articles

Aguirre, Luis Perez. "Breaking the Cycle of Evil" in *Fellowship* 60 (July/Aug. 1994).

Burgess, John P. "Church in East Germany Helps Create *die Wende*" in *The Christian Century* 106 (6 Dec. 1989): 1140-42.

Burgess, John P. "Church-State Relations in East Germany: The Church as a 'Religious' and 'Political' Force" in *Journal of Church and Society* (1990), 17-35.

"Church and Stasi" in *The Christian Century* 109 (Jan. 29, 1992): 89.

Conway, John S. "The Political Role of German Protestantism" in *Journal of Church and State* 34 (1992): 819-41.

Conway, John S. "The *Stasi* and the Churches: Between Coercion and Compromise in East German Protestantism, 1949-89" in *Journal of Church and State* 36 (1992): 725-45.

Darbo Lietuva (*Labor Lithuania*) Kaunas, Summer 1940.

"Genocide and Resistance" in *Journal of Genocide and Resistance in Lithuania 1999-2000*.

Gray, Paul. "*Waves from the Past*" in *Time* 47 (March, 1995).

Howard, Jarvis. "A Crisis of Faith" in *The Baltics World Wide*, 6 Vilnius (1997).

Howard, Jarvis. "An Interview with Father Algis Gudaitis" in *The Baltics World Wide*, 7 Vilnius (1999).

Jeffrey, Paul. "Telling the Truth" in *The Christian Century* 112 (30 Aug.-6 Sep. 1995).

Krieger, David. "Law, Reconciliation, and Peacemaking." *Fellowship* 61 (July/Aug. 1995).

Lietuvos kardinolas, arkivyskupas ir vyskupai (Lithuanian Bishops Conference). "Kuriant brolišką ir laisvą Lietuvą: Lietuvos vyskupų ganytojinis laiškas (Establishing a Brotherly and Free Lithuania: Lithuanian Bishops' Pastoral Letter) in "*Lietuvos aidas*, No. 176 (6134), (09 September 1992): 1 and 5.

Meacham, Carl E. "The Role of the Chilean Catholic Church in the New Chilean Democracy" in *Journal of Church and State* 36 (Spring 1994) (Y 277-99).

153

"Ričardas Jakutis nuteistas pusseptintų metų kalėti" in *Lietuvos Aidas* 95 (18 May 1999) (7842).

Rojas, Fernando Aliaga. "No Impunity in Chile" in *Reconciliation International* 11 (June 1996).

Pastoral Letter of Polish Bishops, October 1995.

Streikus, Arūnas. "Arkivyskupo Teofiliaus Matulionio Santykiai su Sovietine Valdžia 1956 – 1962m," in *Metraštis XII*. Vilnius: Katalikų Akademija, 1998.

Streikus, Arūnas. "Lietuvos Katalikų Bažnyčia 1940 – 1990m," in *Metraštis XII*, Vilnius: Katalikų Akademija, 1998.

Sawatsky, Walter. "Truth Telling in Eastern Europe" in *Journal of Church and Society* 33 (1991): 701-29.

Villa-Vicencio, Charles. "The Road to Reconciliation" in *Sojourners* 26 (May-June, 1997): 34-38.

Volf, Miroslav. "The Social Meaning of Reconciliation." *Journal of Religion in Eastern Europe*, Vol. XVIII (1998): 19-33.

Zalaquett, Jose. "Chile" in *Dealing with the Past*. Boraine, Alex, Levy, Janet & Scheffer, Ronel (eds.) Cape Town: IDASA, 1994.

Ž., A. a.k.a. Spengla V. "LKB Kronikos ištakos, jos balsas Lietuvoje ir pasaulyje," Upublished Manuscript, 2002.

ABOUT THE AUTHOR

Rimantas Gudelis was born in Panevėžys, Lithuania in 1964. He holds a B.A. in Theology from Vytautas Magnus University in Kaunas, Lithuania (1990), an M.A. in Pastoral Theology from Catholic Theological Union (2000), and a Doctorate of Ministry from Catholic Theological Union (2002). From 1990 until 1997 he served as a Roman Catholic priest of the diocese of Panevėžys, Lithuania, and served in different places as associate pastor and pastor. He was responsible for the renovation of the former Communist Pioneer Youth Camp in Berčiūnai, Lithuania, creating Catholic programs there and rebuilding the church dynamited by the Soviets on the campsite. From 1997 until 2001, he served as associate pastor of the Lithuanian parish Nativity of the Blessed Virgin Mary in Chicago, Illinois.